ON PLEASING THE HEAVENLY BRIDEGROOM

by
DALE M. YOCUM

SCHMUL PUBLISHING COMPANY
NICHOLASVILLE, KENTUCKY

COPYRIGHT © 1995 BY ILENE YOCUM.
All rights reserved. No part of this publication may be reproduced or used in any form or by any means—graphic, electronic, or mechanical, including photocopying, recording, taping, or information storage or retrieval systems—without prior written permission of the publishers.

Churches and other noncommercial interests may reproduce portions of this book without prior written permission of the publisher, provided such quotations are not offered for sale—or other compensation in any form—whether alone or as part of another publication, and provided that the text does not exceed 500 words or five percent of the entire book, whichever is less, and does not include material quoted from another publisher. When reproducing text from this book, the following credit line must be included: "From *On Pleasing the Heavenly Bridegroom* by Dale M. Yocum, © 1995 by Ilene Yocum. Used by permission."

Published by Schmul Publishing Co.
PO Box 776
Nicholasville, KY USA

Printed in the United States of America

ISBN 10: 0-88019-332-8
ISBN 13: 978-0-88019-332-0

Visit us on the Internet at www.wesleyanbooks.com, or order direct from the publisher by calling 800-772-6657, or by writing to the above address.

Contents

	PAGE
Jeweled Adornments	5
Separation From the World	14
The Beginnings of Rings	30
The Signet Ring	33
The Signet in Israel	36
Pagan Practices With Rings	39
Why Rings Were Worn	42
The Magic Fascination of the Ring	45
Rings of Love and Betrothal	48
Origin of the Wedding Ring	51
The Use of Symbols	54
God's Jewels	57
The Symbol of Purity	60
The Misuse of Jewelry	63
God's View of Human Jewelry	67
Laws About Rings	70
The Ring in Church History	73
The Ring Rolls On	76
The Holiness Movement and the Ring	79
The Holiness Position and the Ring	82
Some Objections Considered	85
Another Objection	88
The Prodigal	91
Treasures of God's Heart and Hand	94

Jeweled Adornments

Historically the various holiness groups have stood almost unanimously from their beginnings against the wearing of ornamental jewelry. In more recent years some of the groups have dropped their opposition to such practice, thus bringing into question the reasons for their initial opposition.

The Pagan Origin

One thing is certain: although the exact beginnings of human adornment with jewelry cannot be traced, they came from a pagan background. Sacred and secular writers alike witness to the fact. In fact there is strong evidence for the belief that Satan himself originated the custom, and that his fall was partially brought about by that action. He was placed in Eden as guardian of God's dwelling place—a place adorned with symbols of His majesty and holiness. Satan took those symbols to himself to accent his own beauty, and fell as a consequence. According to many commentators Ezek. 28:12-17 speaks of the event. "Thou hast been in Eden the garden of God; every precious stone was thy covering, the sardius, topaz, and the diamond, the beryl, the onyx, and the jasper, the sapphire, the emerald, and the carbuncle, and gold. . . . Thou hast sinned: therefore I will cast thee as profane out of the mountain of God: and I will destroy thee, O covering cherub, from the midst of the stones of fire. Thine heart was lifted up because of thy beauty, thou hast corrupted thy wisdom by reason of thy brightness: I will cast thee to the ground." The Septuagint version says that he covered himself with the precious stones.

From the time of the creation of man, it has been Satan's purpose to plant the seeds of his own sinfulness in human hearts. Could this not well explain why it appears to have been from the beginning an almost uncontrollable human urge to apply jewels and precious stones to the flesh?

This writer had the privilege of visiting the National Museum in Alexandria, Egypt, as well as one in Cairo. There were viewed what are perhaps the oldest finger rings in existence today, dating from the time of the ancient Pharaohs. They were signet rings, used for certifying documents. Prior to finger rings, signets were cylinders suspended around the arm or wrist by a cord. This type was very prominent in Bible lands even after Egypt had finger rings.

It was from Egypt that the idea of a ring as symbol of endless existence came. There seemed to be a strong desire to gain immortality, and along with construction of the pyramids—most ancient buildings known—and embalming of their dead, the ring was also an expression of desire for things that are everlasting. They did not know the true God, and were seeking another way to endless life.

Recognizing the beauty and value of precious stones in finger rings, those ancient kings and princes quickly began to use them for other purposes than signets. Magic powers began to be attributed to them. Some were supposed to bring healing for diseases. Others were time-keepers, a sort of sundial. Certain types were believed to have power over demon spirits, and to guarantee success to the wearer in any venture undertaken. They insured love, health and the fulfillment of every wish, it was believed. King Xerxes had a ring with a carving of a nude woman, the Persian goddess of fertilization. And one of Egypt's kings had a ring with the inscription, "Beautiful God, Conqueror of All Lands." Rings were thus substitutes for God Himself, and were believed to bring all the benefits that the most powerful God could bring.

As jewelry began to creep in among God's chosen people, it was commonly associated with decline into other pagan practices. Passages such as Gen. 35:4; Ex. 32:20, 33:5-6; Ezek. 23:26-44; Jer. 4:30 and Hosea 2:13 show the identification with idolatry and harlotry as well as drunkenness.

The Biblical Condemnation

Numerous passages could be cited which show God's displeasure with jeweled adornment of the flesh. A few cases must suffice. When Jacob took his family back to Bethel, the place where God first met him, he exhorted his family to put away their false gods and their jewels and to bury them under an oak tree. Note that the jewelry was placed in the same category with idols (Gen. 35:4).

When God came to the people of Israel and found them worshiping a golden calf, He showed His anger by requiring that the calf be ground to powder, a large number of the people slain, and all of the jewelry of the people be put off from them (Ex. 32:19, 28; 33: 4-6).

The following passages show the identification which God makes of jewelry and the painted face with harlotry and idolatry:

Speaking of Israel's apostasy, He said, "I will visit upon her the days of Baalim, wherein she burned incense to them, and she decked herself with her earrings and her jewels, and she went after her lovers, and forgat me" (Hos. 2:13).

"Though thou clothest thyself with crimson, though thou deckest thee with ornaments of gold, though thou rentest thy face with painting, in vain shalt thou make thyself fair; thy lovers will despise thee, they will seek thy life" (Jer. 4:30).

"When they had slain their children to their idols, then they came the same day into my sanctuary to profane it. . . . Ye have sent for men to come from far, unto whom a messenger was sent; and, lo, they came: for whom thou didst wash thyself, paintedst thy eyes, and deckedst thyself with ornaments, and satest upon a stately bed. . . . Yet they went in unto her, as they go in unto a woman that playeth the harlot" (Ezek. 23:39-41, 44).

St. Paul and St. Peter both give commandments concerning wearing of jewelry which from the early days of the church have been taken as firm prohibitions applying to all believers. Paul wrote, "I will therefore that . . . women adorn themselves in modest apparel, with shamefacedness and sobriety; not with broided hair, or gold, or pearls, or costly array, but (which becometh women professing godliness) with good works" (I Tim. 2:8-10).

St. Peter's exhortation is as follows, speaking of Christian wives: "Whose adorning let it not be that outward adorning of plaiting the hair, and of wearing of gold, or of putting on of apparel . . ." (I Pet. 3:3). Early church fathers interpreted these passages as prohibitions of jeweled adornment. Wedding rings were not worn until after the close of the Biblical canon, so of course they are not specifically mentioned in Scripture. Many church groups, including virtually all the early holiness bodies, agreed in the application of these scriptures.

The change to permissiveness did not come first through a reinterpretation of Biblical statements, but due to popular pressures. The Roman Catholics finally gave permission for the wedding ring after 700 years of prohibitions, then after another 100 years gave a sacred meaning to the ring, borrowing it from the pagan Egyptians, who had said the ring was a symbol of eternity.

Modern holiness groups have often followed the same course. Their members have insisted on wearing rings, including the wedding ring, and leaders of the groups have become permissive rather than to withstand the public pressure. Reinterpretations of scripture have followed the permissiveness rather than preceding it.

Here are the common interpretations of the last two passages above: 1) The exhortation is not to total abstinence, but to moderation; and 2) Peter's words can not mean abstinence, for they apply to "putting on of apparel" as well as "wearing of gold." In response both of these interpretations can be shown to be exceedingly weak. 1) Whenever St. Peter uses the expression "not . . . but . . ." (*ou . . . alla . . .* in Greek), in every other passage it clearly indicates a total exclusion of the one in favor of the other. For example he says, "Ye know that ye were *not* redeemed with corruptible things, . . . *but* with the precious blood of Christ" (I Pet. 1:18-19). "Being born again, *not* of corruptible seed, *but* of incorruptible, by the word of God, which liveth and abideth forever." (I. Pet. 1:23). It is only reasonable then to interpret this passage in the same way, as meaning a total exclusion of ornamental jewelry from the flesh. 2) Peter does include "putting on of apparel" as one of his prohibitions. However, the word for apparel does not mean all clothing. Looking at St. Paul's instructions we note two different terms used: "modest apparel" and "costly array." The first is commanded, the second forbidden. The word St. Peter uses is the same as Paul's for "array." Vine says it means "an outer garment, a mantle, thrown over the *chiton*." The *chiton* was a complete garment, such as Jesus' seamless coat or tunic (*Vine's Expository Dictionary of New Testament Words,* I, 190). So Peter was speaking about an excessive adornment in dress as St. Paul was in his prohibition.

It is commonly objected that the Bible, in a number of places, seems to approve the wearing of jewelry. Observe four examples with explanations. "And it came to pass . . . that the man took a golden earring of half a shekel weight, and two bracelets for her hands of ten shekels weight of gold" (Gen. 24:22). Abraham's servant had gone to seek a wife for Isaac, and when he found Rebekah he presented her with items of jewelry. It must be remembered that at this time God had not given His laws or expressed His will concerning jewelry. As Paul said much later concerning the worshiping of gold and silver images in Athens, "And the times of this ignorance God winked at; but now commandeth all men everywhere to repent" (Acts 17:29, 30). If God did not rebuke idolatry in every Old Testament instance, it is not surprising if He did not always rebuke other pagan practices.

"And Pharaoh took off his ring from his hand, and put it on Joseph's hand, and arrayed him in vestures of fine linen, and put a gold chain about his neck" (Gen. 41:42). The former observations are pertinent here. In addition it may be commented that the ring put on Joseph's hand was a signet, used for sealing documents, and not a decorative finger ring. Many of the ancient signets were cylinders carried around the wrist, and the term "hand" included the wrist. Even if it may have been a finger ring, it is certain that it was used as a badge of authority.

The ring placed on the hand of the prodigal (Luke 15:22) was of the same sort, an item of authority and family privilege. In Bible lands, much later than in Egypt, the signets were worn around the wrist; and the prodigal's ring was probably of this type. Even if it were a finger ring, it is well to remember that parables are not meant to be followed in every detail as teaching principles. The fact that a "fatted calf" was slain for the feast is not meant to violate the Old Testament rule against eating fat. And the placing of the "best robe" on him was not meant to teach opposite practice from St. Paul's prohibition of "costly array," in I Tim. 2:10. When Jesus said, "And the lord commended the unjust steward, because he had done wisely" (Luke 16:8), He was not approving the injustice involved. He was rather using a parable involving familiar items and events to teach an important truth about foresight. The parable of the prodigal is of the same sort. It teaches that "there is joy in the presence of the angels of God over one sinner that repenteth," a truth illustrated three times in Luke 15.

God spoke of Israel as His unfaithful bride, in Ezek. 16:11-17, when He said, "I decked thee also with ornaments, and I put bracelets upon thy hands, and a chain on thy neck. And I put a jewel on thy forehead, and earrings in thine ears, and a beautiful crown upon thy head. Thus wast thou decked with gold and silver. . . . And thy renown went forth among the heathen for thy beauty: for it was perfect through my comeliness, which I had put upon thee, saith the Lord God. But thou didst trust in thine own beauty, and playedst the harlot. . . . Thou hast also taken thy fair jewels of my gold and of my silver, which I had given thee, and madest thyself images of men." This is highly figurative language, of course. Its meaning is explained by Adam Clarke, with other commentators agreeing: "By this wretched infant, the low estate of the Jewish nation in its origin is pointed out; . . . by her being decked out and ornamented, her Tabernacle service and religious ordinances; by her betrothing and consequent marriage, the covenant which God made with the Jews."

Remember that God appointed the symbolism of precious jewels from the beginning. They represent His own majesty, glory, eternity and holiness. When God has appeared on earth the place of His presence has been beautified with such jewels. (See Gen. 2:12; Ex. 24:10, 17; 28:2, 36; II Chr. 3:5-10; Rev. 21:10-11, 18-21, as examples.) Whereas the pagan nations, and Israel at times, literally put jewels on the flesh, God pointed to the symbolism which such jewels are meant to convey and referred to ". . . my comeliness, which I had put upon thee." They had misused His symbols, as He stated to them: "Thou hast taken *thy* fair jewels of *my* gold and of *my* silver, which I had given thee, and madest *thyself* images . . ." (emphasis added). To misuse God's jewels for fleshly adornment is like misusing His holy name in careless profanity. God's name represents what He is. So do His jewels. Neither should be misused.

In none of the foregoing passages, or in any other, does God recommend or approve the putting of jewels upon the flesh. When it is considered how many times such adornment is condemned in the Word, there should be no hesitancy in recognizing the overall teaching of the Bible.

Changing Church Positions

The injunctions of St. Paul and St. Peter, quoted above, were taken quite generally by the early church fathers as prohibiting the wearing of jewelry. Some made stronger statements than others, but here are samples of those who stood strongly against jeweled adornment:

"If it is necessary for us, while engaged in public business, or discharging other avocations in the country, and often away from our wives, to seal anything for the sake of safety, He (the Word) allows us a signet for this purpose only. Other finger-rings are to be cast off, since according to the Scripture 'instruction is a golden ornament for a wise man' " (Clement of Alexandria, 150-217 A.D., in *Ante-Nicene Fathers,* Vol. II).

"The characteristics of ornaments, and of garments, and the allurements of beauty, are not fitting for any but prostitutes and immodest women; and the dress of none is more precious than of those whose modesty is lowly. Thus in the Holy Scriptures, by which the Lord wished us to be both instructed and admonished, the harlot city is described more beautifully arrayed and adorned, and with her ornaments; and the rather on account of those very ornaments about to perish. . . . Let chaste and modest virgins avoid the dress of the unchaste, the manners of the immodest, the ensigns of brothels, the ornaments of harlots" (Cyprian of Carthage in the early third century, in *Ibid.*).

Not only churches but whole nations passed laws against the wearing of rings in particular, because jewelry was considered as wasteful and conducive to senseless vanity. When the wedding ring appeared in the second century there were laws passed against the use of it. The Roman Catholic Church stood against its use for over 700 years before popular pressure effected a removal of the ban. It was still later that the symbol of unending love was introduced as a means of making sacred what had formerly been viewed as pagan.

Among the churches that stood against jewelry, including the wedding ring, were the Episcopalians, Puritans of England, some Baptists, Congregationalists, Anabaptists, Mennonites and Quakers.

In the beginning of the modern Holiness Movement, John Wesley forbade the wearing of jewelry, including the wedding ring, by members of the Methodist bands. It was because of the gradual relaxation of standards of separation from the world by the Methodist Church, at least in large measure, that a number of holiness bodies had their beginnings in the last part of the 19th century. Quotations could be taken from their writings to show that they almost unanimously stood against ornamental jewelry, on scriptural as well as practical grounds. A. L. Vess wrote,

"Whatever else may be affirmed or denied, one thing is certain: there *was* a time when the jewelry question was settled in the Holiness movement. There was no question as to our stand on the subject, not even the wedding ring was excepted" *(The Loophole)*. Due to popular pressure, however, one after another of these groups has relaxed its opposition; and like the nations and churches of old has found that regulations are ineffective against the natural inclination to adorn the flesh. Dr. George F. Kunz has declared, "The wearing of rings as ornaments for the hand requires no explanation in view of the innate love of adornment shown from the very earliest periods of human history" *(Rings for the Finger)*. Other secular writers have confirmed that it has been a quite universal urge to adorn the flesh with jewels. This is not surprising when we consider the inborn character of inherited sinfulness and the lusts of the flesh.

What is commonly called the "Conservative Holiness Movement" has sought to withstand the slide toward permissiveness by teaching and preaching about the dangers of compromise and lowering of standards of separation from the world. It is not surprising, considering the history of such restraints, if again there appears a popular opposition to them. It is in part because of this danger that the present series of studies is being prepared, so that our people can understand the reasons for carefulness and the dangers of lowering standards.

It is evident from a study of history that when such standards are weakened, there comes in a flood of permissiveness which applies to far more than just one or two simple items. The point of contention may at first be just a wedding ring, or some other single item. Once a concession is made, however, there quickly follows a host of other issues, each as apparently innocent as the first. All put together, though, constitute a deluge that overflows the boundaries; and soon apostasy is sweeping on without restraint. Let us resolve to be safe, careful and restrained in all such matters. It pays to be slow in making changes, lest they contribute to a careless abandonment of sound principles of separation.

Separation From the World

(II Corinthians 6:11—7:1)

The Apostle Paul had more to say about the world in his letters to the Corinthian believers than in any other of his writings, and for good reason. Corinth was a city beset by the worst kinds of debauchery and immorality. The young church there had not come to the place of purity and stability through the sanctifying grace of God. So the Apostle warned repeatedly about being absorbed by this present world. He spoke of the wisdom of this world, which is foolishness with God (I Cor. 1:20); the princes of this world that come to nought (2:6); the spirit of this world, which believers do not possess (2:12); using the world, but not abusing it (7:31); the fashion of the world, which passeth away (7:31); the condemnation of the world, which the Lord seeks to deliver us from (11:32); the god of this world, who blinds the minds of unbelievers (II Cor. 4:4); and much more.

That there must be a real and practical separation between the Church and the world, St. Paul argued from the fact that there can be nothing in common between them. He presented five irreconcilable differences, in II Cor. 6:14-16, "What fellowship hath righteousness with unrighteousness? and what communion hath light with darkness? And what concord hath Christ with Belial? or what part hath he that believeth with an infidel? And what agreement hath the temple of God with idols? for ye are the temples of the living God."

Fellowship means a common CAUSE, and there is no common cause between righteousness and unrighteousness. *Communion* means a common USE or employment, and there is no common employment of light and darkness. *Concord* literally means a common MUSIC or symphony, and there is no common music between Christ and Belial. How could Christ and the devil possibly harmonize with their kinds of music? *Part* means a common division (of land), or a common DESTINY, and there is no common destiny between the believer and the infidel. Finally, *Agreement* means a common COMMITMENT, and there is no common commitment between the temple of God and idols. One is the habitation of God; the other is identified with demons. There is just no overlapping of the two!

It is impossible to love this present world system and to love God at the same time. Nobody can be both a friend of the world and a friend of God at the same time (I John 2:15; James 4:4).

The Landmarks of Separation

The word St. Paul selected to use for separation means "to mark off from others by boundaries" (Thayer's *Greek Lexicon*, p. 90). When he said, "come out from among them, and be ye separate, saith the Lord," he was drawing an analogy between the church in her separation from the world, and Israel in her separation from the heathen nations which surrounded her. There were literal boundaries drawn to mark off the land of Israel from other nations. Commonly they were called landmarks. It is instructive to compare them with the lines of separation between the church and the world.

Those ancient landmarks were set by God Himself. He said to His chosen people, "I will set thy bounds from the Red sea even unto the sea of the Philistines, and from the desert even unto the river" (Ex. 23:31). Those boundaries were also set by the fathers. Prov. 22:28 states, "Remove not the ancient landmark, which thy fathers have set." God indicated the primary positions—"cornerposts" as it were—and the fathers placed special marker stones along the borders between the corners. Finally, each landowner had to use wisdom in deciding where the line was between the marker stones.

Separation from the world is established in the same way. Some things God has settled forever in His Word. For example,

Jesus set forth some attitudes of the Gentiles which His people are not to manifest. They include preoccupation and anxiety concerning food, drink and clothing (Matt. 6:32), and aspiration to authority instead of service (Matt. 20:25). These are fixed landmarks! There are actions specified also, which are forever off limits for the Christian: fornication, evil speaking, thievery, slothfulness, and many more. These are not open for debate. God has established them, and they are not to be moved.

In addition to those fixed points of moral separation, new issues arise from time to time for which the Bible does not give a ready answer. Tobacco is never mentioned. Neither is television watching, nor test-tube babies, nor pant suits, nor a lot of other issues that confront modern society. This does not mean that there is no guidance available. Just as the Israelite fathers placed stone markers between the corners, spiritual leaders are responsible for helping to find sound answers, consistent with God's Word. Hebrews 13:17 exhorts, "Obey them that have the rule over you, and submit yourselves: for they watch for your souls, as they that must give account, that they may do it with joy, and not with grief: for that is unprofitable for you." Lest this should develop blind acceptance of just anybody's teachings, the writer gives some precautions: "Be not carried about with divers and strange doctrines" (v. 9); and "Remember them which have the rule over you, who have spoken unto you the word of God: whose faith follow, considering the end of their conversation" (v. 7). Kenneth Wuest translates the last clause thus: "whose faith imitate as you closely observe the outcome of their manner of life." Measure their teachings by the Word as far as possible; and follow them only as their life progresses toward more of godliness and not more of worldliness.

There is a modern teaching, which is rapidly gaining popularity, that tradition is a needless imposition and should be set aside; further, that where the Bible does not specifically forbid a certain action, the individual is free to follow his own inclinations relative to that action. Both positions need to be exposed for the dangerous error which they contain.

Relative to tradition, it is true that Jesus rebuked the scribes and Pharisees because they had exalted their traditions to as high a position as the Scriptures of God. He said, "Thus have ye made the commandment of God of none effect by your tradition. . . . In vain they do worship me, teaching for doctrines the commandments of men: (Matt. 15:6, 9). Jesus was not condemning tradition as such, but the elevation of tradition above the Scripture, and even in contradiction of it. That tradition has a proper place we must conclude from the command of St. Paul, "Therefore, brethren, stand fast, and hold the traditions which ye have been taught, whether by word, or our epistle" (II Thess. 2:15). When godly men have stood together effectively for a position of separation from the world, while maintaining an empowered witness before the world, such tradition should not be replaced unless there is a more effective way of maintaining separation while bearing witness for Christ. If the removal of tradition is simply a means of reducing the level of separation from the world, it surely must be placed in the category of friendship with the world, and that is soundly condemned in the Word of God.

With regard to the second position, that one is free to do anything not specifically forbidden in the Word, the falsity of such teaching is obvious on careful consideration. Cigarette smoking is not forbidden in the Word; neither is child pornography, nor gambling, nor a lot of other issues that are of the utmost significance. If one is to argue that we are without divine guidance in such issues, it means that God has left "every man to do what is right in his own eyes," in an extremely complex age. This is simply not the case. Bible scholars are able to provide principles *based on God's Word,* though *not specifically declared in it,* which apply to all the above issues. To set aside such teaching as worthless tradition is to violate the passage from Heb. 13:17, quoted above.

To insist that people are free to do everything not specifically forbidden in the Word is no more justifiable than to insist they are prevented from doing everything not specifically commanded in the Word. The fact is, the Bible does not uphold either position. It declares, "Whether therefore ye eat, or drink, or whatsoever ye do, do all to the glory of God" (I Cor. 10:31). The modern teachers would have to reword that passage to read, "Whatsoever ye do, do all to please yourself, except where the Bible gives specific commandment." I John 3:22 states, "Whatsoever we ask, we receive of him, because we keep his commandments, and do those things that are pleasing in his sight." It would have to be rewritten, "we keep his commandments and then do those things that are pleasing in our own sight." The "not" would have to be omitted from Rom. 15:1, "We then that are strong ought to bear the infirmities of the weak, and not to please ourselves."

The fact is that this modern emphasis on self-pleasing is very close to the tactic of Satan when he persuaded Eve in the Garden, "ye shall be as gods, knowing good and evil" (Gen. 3:5). He wanted her to feel perfectly capable of making moral judgments for herself, without reference to the guidance of God. The modern teaching even puts God on the same side as Satan, when it declares, "God wants you to do whatever you desire, and whatever makes you feel good." There is no such teaching in the Bible. It commands, "Trust in the Lord with all thine heart: and lean not unto thine own understanding. In all thy ways acknowledge him, and he shall direct thy paths" (Prov. 3:5, 6). It says, "Go to now, ye that say, Today or tomorrow we will go into such a city, and continue there a year, and buy and sell and get gain: and do this or that" (James 4:13, 15). No mortal person knows enough to find his own way through the moral issues of these days without intimate guidance from God. To declare personal independence to do just as one pleases, a part from specific commandments, is to plead for the central root of sin: pleasing oneself. That sin must be purged if one is to be a totally committed love-slave to Jesus Christ!

Finally, there are points which the individual must decide, under the guidance of the Holy Spirit. Concerning such matters as keeping special days holy unto the Lord, Paul said, "One man esteemeth one day above another: another esteemeth every day alike. Let every man be fully persuaded in his own mind" (Rom. 12:5; the entire chapter is excellent for study in this matter). The whole discussion is given on the assumption of a sincere faith in Christ, and is not a justification for unprincipled self-seeking. Each position concerning the holy days is "unto the Lord," the Apostle insists.

The Law of Separation

"Having therefore these promises, dearly beloved, let us cleanse ourselves from all filthiness of the flesh and spirit, perfecting holiness in the fear of God" (II Cor. 7:1). In making his appeal for perfected holiness, the Apostle refers to a set of three promises he had quoted from the Old Testament: Lev. 26:12; Isa. 52:11; and Ex. 4:22. The first and last related to Israel's coming out of Egypt into the Holy Land, and assured them that if they left the practices of Egypt behind and kept God's holy law, He would dwell among them in His tabernacle, and would give them unprecedented blessings. The second promise related to Israel's future return from Babylon, and commanded them to return without touching any of the uncleanness of that pagan land. God would then go before them and behind them, protecting them from danger.

In applying these promises to the Church, St. Paul commanded a cleansing from "all filthiness of the flesh and spirit." There are no physical boundaries between the Church and the world to be maintained, but there are just as real principles of separation that affect flesh and spirit—attitudes, conduct and appearance. The spirit must be purged from its affinity for the world, and the flesh must be purged from the enslavement of worldly lusts.

Tracing the analogy between Israel and the Church in their separation, the use of the word "filthiness" has much significance. In the Old Testament it applied especially to four great sins to which Israel was inclined, and which identified them with the pagan world about them.

The first was idolatry. In Ezek. 36:25 the Lord said, "Then will I sprinkle clean water upon you, and ye shall be clean: from all your filthiness, and from all your idols, will I cleanse you. A new heart will I give you, and a new spirit will I put within you . . . and cause you to walk in my statutes." Israel was perpetually inclined to accept the religious practices of Egypt, or of the surrounding nations; and God always soundly condemned them for it. In our culture the problem is not bowing down to images of wood and stone, but of a more subtle form of idolatry. In Col. 3:5 St. Paul stated that covetousness is idolatry. It is one of the most subtle sins there is, yet God equates it with idolatry. St. Paul had thought he was a perfect keeper of the law until God showed him that he was covetous (Rom. 7:7-9). He thought he was trying to please God, but found that in all things he was really pleasing himself. When he recognized his sinfulness he groaned within himself until he found deliverance in Christ Jesus. Here are some questions that point to a covetous heart: Do you have a subtle desire to please yourself, or do you have a fervent passion to please God in all things? Do you put material things ahead of spiritual things in your conversation, your plans, your joys? Do you let the job crowd out your time for devotion? Will you violate the Lord's day for [if you get] enough money or pleasure? Would you sell liquor and tobacco, and would you cheat a little, for a good raise in pay?

The second sin was adultery, which was often connected with idolatry as an act of pagan worship. God condemned Israel thus: "And one hath committed abominations with his neighbor's wife. . . . And I will scatter thee among the nations, and disperse thee in the countries, and will consume thy filthiness out of thee" (Ezek. 22:11, 15). Israel was considered the wife of Jehovah. When she went after the heathen, following their practices, God charged her with adultery. Likewise the Church is the bride of Christ, and when she becomes a friend of the world, she is charged with adultery. James said, "Ye adulterers and adulteresses, know ye not that the friendship of the world is enmity against God? whosoever therefore will be a friend of the world is the enemy of God" (Jas. 4:4).

James did not give specific definition of friendship, in terms of practices involved; and that is perhaps good, for the expression of such friendship changes from age to age, and from culture to culture. Surely one of the evidences of friendship today is the religious idea that believers must become more like the world as an aid in winning them to Christ. That was the error of Nicolas, the proselyte of Antioch, one of the first deacons, according to Bible commentators. Jesus said He hated that doctrine, and so should we (Rev. 2:6, 15. See also Acts 6:5). Winning people for Christ is not a matter of mere human approach, although that is vital. It involves a divine visitation by the Spirit, as Peter asserted: "Have your conversation honest among the Gentiles; that, whereas they speak against you as evildoers, they may by your good works, which they shall behold, glorify God in the day of visitation" (I Pet. 2:12).

The third mark of filthiness was drunkenness. In Isa. 28:7-8 God's people were condemned once more: "But they also have erred through wine, and through strong drink are out of the way; the priest and the prophet have erred through strong drink, they are swallowed up on wine, they are out of the way through strong drink; they err in vision, they stumble in judgment. For all tables are full of vomit and filthiness, so that there is no place clean." What a vivid description of the calamity of strong drink, and its influence on people's actions and decisions! The habit is no less filthy today. God condemns it now just as He did for Israel. Paul commanded in Eph. 5:18, "Be not drunk with wine, wherein is excess; but be filled with the Spirit."

The fourth mark was pride and fleshly adornment by the daughters of Zion. Again the words are from Isaiah, in 4:3-4, "He that remaineth in Jerusalem shall be called holy, . . . when the Lord shall have washed away the filth of the daughters of

Zion, and shall have purged the blood of Jerusalem from the midst thereof by the spirit of judgment, and by the spirit of burning." (Here is a clear allusion to a double cleansing that yields holiness: an outward washing by water, and an inward purging by fire.) To see what the filthiness of the daughter of Zion was it is necessary to go back into Chapter 3, where there is a detailed analysis of a twofold filthiness: haughtiness of spirit (v. 16), and adornments and display of the flesh (vv. 16-24). There are some details that would be very difficult to understand today; others have an exact counterpart in modern fleshly show: rings, bracelets, earrings, and ornaments of the legs, for example. God labeled these specifically as filthiness, and declared they needed cleansing. St. Paul translated the same emphasis into the New Testament teaching about cleansing and holiness, as our Scripture portion illustrates.

Lest any reader thinks this interpretation is forcing an Old Testament situation inappropriately upon a New Testament passage, consider a quotation from the last book of the New Testament, Rev. 17:4-6, "The woman was arrayed in purple and scarlet colour, and decked with gold and precious stones and pearls, having a golden cup in her hand full of abominations and filthiness of her fornication: and upon her forehead was a name written, MYSTERY, BABYLON THE GREAT, THE MOTHER OF HARLOTS AND ABOMINATIONS OF THE EARTH. And I saw the woman drunken with the blood of the saints, and with the blood of the martyrs of Jesus." Commentators quite agree that this woman represents all false religions, including idolatry (abominations), and that she is joined in league with the Antichrist. All four of the Old Testament marks of filthiness appear here, clustered around the word "filthiness" which is used in verse 4. There is idolatry, included with the abominations, fornication, drunkenness and jewelry. Though the woman represents religion, as did the daughters of Zion, it is a kind of religion that God stoutly rejects. He demands either purging or destruction.

According to the Old Testament law, if Israel would maintain careful separation from pagan practices and alliances, God promised to give them peace, fruitfulness, victory over every foe, increase in number, security, the revealed presence of God, and more. (Read Lev. 26, as one example of God's conditional promise.) St. Paul applied the same promises to the church, with particular emphasis on sonship to God.

The Loss of Separation

In spite of all God's promises and warnings, there seemed to be an irresistible seduction that kept drawing Israel back to pagan relationships, until they finally were sent into captivity as a judgment from God. Occasionally revival would come, and the separation be renewed, but the results were not permanent. Carnal leaders canceled out the gains made by the good ones, and the same old seductions appeared again and again.

There were some specific examples which St. Paul chose as warnings for the Church. In I Corinthians, Chapter 10, he gave five illustrations of Israel's backslidings, and then summarized, "Now all these things happened unto them for ensamples: and they are written for our admonition, upon whom the ends of the world are come" (v. 11). Two examples dealt with a loss of separation from the pagan world. The first involved the golden calf at Sinai (Ex. 32). While Moses was in the Mount, the people asked for gods that could lead them, and Aaron, the supreme compromiser, fashioned a god just like they had seen in Egypt. He put an altar to Jehovah in front of it and allowed a combination of divine and heathen worship. At least two of the marks of filthiness were involved there: idolatry and jewelry. It is possible a third was also included, as the "play" and "nakedness to their shame" may have been fornication—a practice so common in idol worship (See Ex. 32:6, 25).

When God spoke His rebuke for the tragic sin, He said He would not go up in the midst of the people, and the tabernacle was removed from the encampment of people. Moses entreated,

"Wherein shall it be known here that I and thy people have found grace in thy sight? Is it not in that thou goest with us? *So shall we be separated,* I and thy people, from all the people that are upon the face of the earth" (33:16. Emphasis added). The Lord required that the idol be totally destroyed, that every bit of jewelry be put away, and that 3000 people be slain before He agreed to go forward in the midst of them. Do you see how important God considered that matter of separation?

Paul's second example referred to the treachery of Balaam (Num. 22-25, 31). He was invited by Balak, king of Moab, to come and curse Israel, with a promise of great honor and reward. God forbade the mission, but Balaam calculated a method that would gain him the reward just as handily, by teaching the Moabites to entice Israel into a compromise of their separation. Numbers 25:1-3 summarizes, "And Israel abode in Shittim, and the people began to commit whoredom with the daughters of Moab. And they called the people unto the sacrifices of their gods: and the people did eat, and bowed down to their gods. And Israel joined himself unto Baal-peor: and the anger of the Lord was kindled against Israel." It was a virtual repeat of the Sinai incident, though committed on foreign ground: idolatry, fornication, and a serious compromise of the borders of separation. This time the judgment was more serious, however, for 24,000 people died in the plague that followed.

The last three New Testament writers—Peter, Jude and John—include warnings against the policy of Balaam as a means of compromising the separation and purity of the Church. In Rev. 2:14-15 is the last mention, included with a condemnation of the policy of Nicolas. Speaking to the church of Pergamos, Jesus said, "I have a few things against thee, because thou hast there them that hold the doctrine of Balaam, who taught Balac to cast a stumblingblock before the children of Israel, to eat things sacrificed unto idols, and to commit fornication. So hast thou also them that hold the doctrine of the Nicolaitans, which thing I hate."

Whenever there are teachers in the church that recommend a lowering of the standard of separation from the world, there are people in the church who are inclined in that direction, and who readily move toward the world in their attitudes, appearance or conduct. It was always so in Israel, and it is not surprising that the carnal hearts of many church members react in the same way. Jesus condemned such teachers, and such followers, in His words to the churches; and that condemnation is just as appropriate now. How important it is to have godly, committed leadership.

Restoration of true separation involves both an inward and outward cleansing. "Let us cleanse ourselves from all filthiness of the flesh and spirit, perfecting holiness in the fear of God" (II Cor. 7:1). Outwardly there must be total removal of the marks of filthiness, whether of idolatry, adultery, drunkenness, jewelry, or any other modern mark of world conformity. Removal of "all filthiness" does not permit a small amount to remain! Inwardly there must be purging from all inclination to love the world, make friends with it, or be conformed to it. We are to love people in the world as Jesus did, in the sense of longing for their recovery from its damning snares. But we are not to envy this lost and depraved world system, or the people who are captured by its fascinations. Christians serve a different Master, walk a higher road, and possess a different destiny!

The Love That Separates

"Holiness in the fear of God"—that is the goal before us, which calls us to pay the price of perfect separation. That phrase, "the fear of God," is used often in the Bible, and it should be a high challenge for every believer. It does not mean fright or panic, but an intense reverence that produces the utmost carefulness to avoid offense. Holiness in the fear of God involves at least three elements. First, there is the *love of God, which is a sufficient motivation.* Moses warned Israel of the danger of their being sent into captivity due to compromise, and said that if they would return to the Lord He would bring them back home again. "And the Lord thy God will circumcise thine heart, and the heart of thy seed, to love the Lord thy God with all thine heart, and with all thy soul, that thou mayest live. . . . And thou shalt return and obey the voice of the Lord, and do all his commandments which I command thee this day" (Deut. 30:6, 8). "Circumcision of the heart" is an Old Testament figure pointing to the complete cleansing from sin which is possible through the blood of Christ. It makes possible such a love for God that obedience to His commands is a delight!

Hear the words of St. Paul as he wrote to the Corinthian believers of his motivations in Christian service: "For the love of Christ constraineth us; because we thus judge, that if one died for all, then were all dead: and that he died for all, that they which live should not henceforth live unto themselves, but unto him which died for them, and rose again. Wherefore henceforth know we no man after the flesh: yea, though we have known Christ after the flesh, yet now henceforth know we him no more" (II Cor. 5:14-16). In the same chapter he said, referring to the judgment seat of Christ, before which every believer must appear, "Knowing therefore the terror of the Lord, we persuade men" (v. 10). He could contemplate the seriousness of judgment, and be an ambassador for Christ, bringing men into reconciliation with God, and do it all from the motivation of love for Christ!

Second, there is the *pleasure of the Lord, which is a sufficient aim.* Jesus summarized His ministry thus: "I do nothing of myself; but as my Father hath taught me, I speak these things. And he that sent me is with me: the Father hath not left me alone; for I do always those things that please him" (John 8:28, 29). The Apostle insisted that we who are followers of Jesus must follow His example. "We beseech you, brethren, and exhort you by the Lord Jesus, that as ye have received of us how ye ought to walk and to please God, so ye would abound more and more" (I Thess. 4:1). When a person is pleasing God, as Enoch did (Heb. 11:5), God testifies to that person of His pleasure, and he will want no higher aim in life than to keep on pleasing his heavenly Father!

Third, there is the *glory of God, which is a sufficient delight*. Some people perpetually seek the glory of this world, which proves vain and disappointing. Could they but once experience the glory of God's blessed presence, they would see how much better it is than the passing excitements of the world, the flesh and the devil. When God came into the temple of old, at its dedication, the people were so overwhelmed by His glory that they fell on their faces in wonder and worship (II Chr. 7:1-3). No sacrifice was too great to offer to a God so glorious! In the passage about the purging of Jerusalem, Isaiah emphasized how important is the glory of God's presence. He said, "The Lord will create upon every dwelling place of Mount Zion, and upon her assemblies, a cloud and smoke by day, and the shining of a flaming fire by night: for upon all the glory shall be a defence" (Isa. 4:5). The glory of God is always the best defense against compromise and apostasy, whether in the dwelling place (the home) or the assembly (the church). Oh, may we keep the glory of God in our homes and churches! But just as at Mt. Sinai, a violation of our separation will cause the glory to depart. Clever human programs and brilliant human achievements may be substituted; and although carnal, undiscerning hearts may be satisfied, God never will be. And after all, it is His pleasure at which we must always aim.

Questions for Research and Discussion

1. Trace all references to "the world" in St. Paul's letters to the Corinthians, and seek to arrive at a good definition of the term.
2. What are some practical applications of the command, "Be ye not unequally yoked together with unbelievers" (II Cor. 6:14)?

3. Consulting scholars and commentaries as necessary, make a distinction between the love of the world (I John 2:15); the lusts of the world (I John 2:17); and the friendship of the world (James 4:4).
4. List several (12-15) of the common practices of this world which are forbidden for the Christian in God's Word. List scripture references.
5. List several moral issues, not mentioned in the Bible, about which godly men have historically agreed in their effort to maintain careful separation from the world. On what passages have they based their stand for separation?
6. Name some issues to be settled within an individual's own conscience, about which there appear to be no scriptural principles that determine a certain position.
7. What are some possible reasons why there is so much talk against "tradition" today? What does the Bible say about it?
8. Using a concordance make a list of the types of conduct which the Bible classes as filthiness, in both Old and New Testaments. (There are some more, in addition to those listed in this chapter.)
9. Why does the Bible call friendship with the world adultery? What analogy is found in the Old Testament? (See Jer. 3, for example.)
10. Aside from the initial account in Numbers, find all you can about what the Bible says concerning Balaam. Why are such strong warnings found in the New Testament?
11. Using commentaries by Richard Barclay and others, find out what is meant by the "doctrine of the Nicolaitans," which the Lord hates (Rev. 2:6, 15).
12. Is "pleasing God" something more than just keeping His commandments? If so, what is the difference? Use scriptures like I John 3:21, 22 in your study.
13. If Israel was to be so strictly separated from the pagan nations, how could they ever bring any of the pagan people to know God? Search passages like Isa. 43:21; Josh. 4:23,

24; I Sam. 17:46; Lev. 19:34; II Chron. 13:18; Isa. 56:4-8; and Esther 8:17.
14. Evaluate the modern teaching that if the church is to win the world, the church must become more like the world. Consider what godly men have said on this subject. Consider the analogy of question 13, and scriptures like I Cor. 9:19-23 (in context); Rom. 15:15-31; Rom. 12:21; Acts 5:11-14 and I Pet. 2:9-12.
15. How have you personally been challenged through this study of separation from the world?

The Beginnings of Rings

Mystery in History

Like the ring itself, the history of ring wearing has no obvious beginning. Rings are supposed to signify a quality of unendingness. There is no certain point in history where it is possible to say the practice began. Obviously there was a beginning, but its location is lost in mystery. The best that can be done is to search in the historical records we have, and in the results of archaeological discovery, to establish something of the ancient practice.

Huge books have been written about the history of the ring, and what is known sheds much light on the wearing of rings today. This study will be directed toward finding out from history how the ring did originate, and what the implications are for us today.

The Bible Record

Several historical records researched for this series indicate that the most ancient references to ring wearing are in the Bible. These are found in Genesis 38:18 and 41:42, "And [Judah] said. What pledge shall I give thee? And she said, Thy signet, and thy bracelets, and thy staff that is in thine hand." "And Pharaoh took off his ring from his hand, and put it upon Joseph's hand, and arrayed him in vestures of fine linen, and put a gold chain about his neck . . . and he made him ruler over all the land of Egypt." (There are earlier references to wearing of bracelets and earrings, but not specifically to rings. (See Gen. 24:22.)

Encyclopedia Britannica commented, "At an early period, when the art of writing was known to but very few, it was commonly the custom for men to wear rings on which some distinguishing sign or badge was engraved, so that by using it as a seal the owner could give a proof of authenticity to letters or other documents. Thus, when some royal personage wished to delegate his power to one of his officials, it was not unusual for him to hand over his signet ring, by means of which the full royal authority could be given to the written commands of the subordinate (cf. Gen. 41:42; Esther 8:2)."

Both of the above references in Genesis could well apply to use of the signet in this way. It is certainly the case when Pharaoh gave his signet to Joseph, and it may well have been so with Judah's signet also. In fact, the word *signet* is derived from its use in signing or sealing the documents and other items which were to be guarded against tampering.

The Form of a Signet

"In ancient Babylonia and Assyria finger rings do not appear to have been used. In those countries the signet took a different form, namely, that of a cylinder cut in crystal or other hard stone, and perforated from end to end. A cord was passed through it, and it was worn on the wrist like a bracelet. This way of wearing the signet is more than once alluded to in the Old Testament (Gen. 38:18, and S. of S. 8:6)" *(Ibid.)*. The latter verse says, "Set me as a seal upon thine heart, as a seal upon thine arm: for love is strong as death." it is upon the arm that the seal was to be placed, and not on a finger. It may be noted that at that early date the binding quality of love had been identified with the sealing of the signet.

That all rings had their origin from the cylindrical signet is indicated by Kunz: "The origin of the ring is somewhat obscure, although there is good reason to believe that it is a modification of the cylindrical seal which was first worn attached to the neck or to the arm and was eventually reduced in size so that it could be worn on the finger" (Dr. George F. Kunz, *Rings for the Finger*). Kunz further indicated that the custom of wearing rings was transmitted from Egypt to the Greeks, and thence to the Etruscans and Romans. Though he did not declare it so specifically, this would appear to indicate that the ring which Pharaoh placed upon Joseph was a cylinder about the wrist. The record says that it was placed upon his hand, not on a finger.

The writer had the rare privilege of visiting the national museum of Egypt, and observing a great assortment of ancient rings taken from tombs of the Pharaohs. Many of them were finger rings, which had signets on them. It is thus certain that at a rather early date signets were adapted to be worn in that way.

Engravings on the Egyptian signets usually included the title and name of the owner written deeply in the metal in hieroglyphic characters. Later Pharaohs used a figure of the scarab (beetle) as their seal, and this became very popular. Many of the rings still in existence have a form of beetle on them.

A Fable of Origin

Pliny, the ancient historian, told a story of how the ring first came to be worn. According to his tale, Prometheus dared to steal some of the fire of heaven and start it burning on earth for human use. For such profanity the god Jupiter sentenced him to be chained to a rock for thirty thousand years while a vulture feasted on his liver. Long before the dire sentence was completed, however, Jupiter relented and set Prometheus free, with one restriction. In order that his sentence might not be considered totally annulled, the prisoner was to have one link of his chain placed forever around his finger, and in it was set a portion of the stone to which he had been bound. Thus technically he could be considered still bound to that very rock.

Obviously those Greeks didn't know for sure how ring wearing got started either.

The Signet Ring

God's Signet

It is well established that the most ancient type of ring historically was the signet ring. The Lord himself referred to its significance when He declared that Judah was to go into captivity. "As I live, saith the Lord, though Coniah the son of Jehoiakim king of Judah were the signet upon my right hand, yet would I pluck thee thence; and I will give thee into the hand of them that seek thy life . . . into the hand of the Chaldeans" (Jer. 22:24, 25). There are two things worthy of note: first, the signet represents value and permanence; second, others than the owner covet to obtain it. Since the signet carries with it the full authority of the rightful owner, it is not strange that it was coveted by those who would like to usurp the authority it signified. It will appear repeatedly in the study that there is a strange and almost overpowering desire to wear a ring.

Britannica stated the desire thus: "To decorate the human finger with a ring, if possible with one combining beauty, value, and a distinctive character, was a widely spread natural impulse."

God's message about the signet is taken up again in Haggai 2:22, 23, "l will overthrow the throne of kingdoms, and will destroy the strength of the kingdoms of the heathen. . . . In that day, saith the Lord of hosts, will take thee, O Zerubbabel, my servant, the son of Shealtiel, saith the Lord, and will make thee as a signet: for I have chosen thee, saith the Lord of hosts."

The signet was surrendered when Judah went into captivity. Now the nation is returned, and God has His signet back in place again. It is a figure of treasured possession. Moreover, it signified the making process: I "will make thee as a signet." On some occasions the image of the owner was carved on the signet. Perhaps this was in God's mind as He spoke the words. Zerubbabel had a great work to do, for he must rebuild the temple of God. To him the Lord said, "Not by might, nor by power, but by my spirit, saith the Lord of hosts" (Zech. 4:6).

It should be observed that by using the figure of a signet, God was not approving any subsequent use that might be made of rings. It was often the case in the Bible that some practice with which people were familiar was utilized to teach an object lesson without any approval being given of the practice involved. For example, when Jesus said, "And the lord commended the unjust steward. because he had done wisely" Luke 16:8), He was not approving the dishonesty involved. He was rather putting a premium on foresight, preparing for future welfare in present calculations.

Engravings of a Signet

The art of signet-making must have been rather common in Bible times, for it is frequently used as a comparison with other engravings. Exodus 39:30 states, for example, "And they made the plate of the holy crown of pure gold, and wrote upon it a writing, like to the engravings of a signet, HOLINESS TO THE LORD." Similar statements are made about the priest's breastplate, the mitre on his forehead, and the shoulder pieces on his garment.

When the signet came to be worn on the finger, there was the metal or stone band which encircled the finger, and the raised, flattened portion called the bezel, in which the carving was made. On its completion the figure on the signet could be impressed in any soft substance that would thereafter harden and leave the permanent imprint, such as clay or wax. That imprint was the mark of authority, just as a signature is today.

The signet was then not an item of adornment, but an essential means of certifying proper authority in the transaction of business.

Pertaining to Kings

A ring was a thing for a king to wear. It did not pertain to common folks, as the signet was a sign of authority which they did not have. Pharaoh gave one to Joseph, and with it transferred some of his own power to rule the people. When Daniel was shut in the den of lions, King Darius sealed the stone covering "with his own signet, and with the signet of his lords" (Dan. 6:17). Not only did the king have a signet then; his lords were given some also, that they might assert their proper measure of authority. But that right and that power came from the king. Concerning these cases Kunz remarked, "Still, these might have been of the well-known Babylonian type of 'rolling seals' and not rings" (Kunz, *Rings for the Finger*).

When Haman secured King Ahasuerus' permission to destroy all the Jews in his kingdom, the king gave his ring to Haman. He in turn allowed the scribes to use it as they sent a letter to every part of the kingdom, "and sealed with the king's ring" (Esther 3:12).

Interestingly, a signet has been found which belonged to King Shishak of Egypt, the monarch who conquered Jerusalem and plundered the Temple about 975 B.C. The ring, housed in the British Museum, has a stone scarab (beetle) mounted on a gold band (II Chron. 12).

Antiochus and the Ring

Ancient records show that Antiochus Epiphanes, the forerunner and type of the antichrist, who persecuted the Jews so cruelly in the second century B.C., conveyed his authority by means of a signet ring. When he approached death, he handed his ring to his trusted counselor, Philip, with instructions that it be kept for Antiochus' son, who was only nine years old at the time. The son only lived two more years, however, so Philip kept the ring and considered it as authority for himself to rule with royal power.

Until this time rings were largely confined to kings, at least so far as signets were concerned. Things were not to remain that way though, as the next study will reveal.

The Signet in Israel

For Utility and for Show

Ring wearing began with use of the signet, as earlier studies have shown. Those signets were first cylinders fastened around the neck or the arm. Gradually a change was made to finger rings with signets on them, used for sealing documents.

It was not long until rings became more than instruments of utility, however. Instead of clay cylinders, rings were made of gold and other precious materials. And these were adorned with increasingly ornate figures and carvings. Precious stones, such as emerald and sardonyx, were set in the base of gold and elaborately carved. The gold base of the bezel (upraised portion) was also carved. The bezel was often attached to the ring in such a way that it could swivel to a desired position for the seal to be applied. One such ring, now preserved in a New York museum, has a scarab (beetle) carefully engraved in a translucent green stone. Around the base are two wrestlers, entirely naked except for a short apron on each. Back of each wrestler is a winged serpent, and between them is an object which is apparently the head of a wolf.

Obviously there was a trend away from mere utility, to more and more of decoration and show.

Dealing With Pagan Issues

The signet ring was of pagan origin. True, there was utility in its original purpose the sealing of official documents. Not everything of pagan origin is inherently evil. Our calendar owes much of its development to the pagan Babylonians, as do other aspects of astronomy.

When Israel came forth from Egypt, where the signet rings originated, jewelry was an issue with them. God instructed Moses that his people should ask jewels of gold and silver from the Egyptians. One purpose was to "spoil the Egyptians" (Ex. 3:22). Another was to have the necessary precious materials for building the Tabernacle (Ex. 35:4-29). Plainly God did not plan for the same use to be made of the items that had been made in Egypt.

After the incident of the golden calf, the Lord spoke and said, "Now put off thy ornaments from thee, that I may know what to do unto thee. And the children of Israel stripped themselves of their ornaments by the mount Horeb" (Ex. 33:5, 6). They might have objected, asserting that these things had utility value. But the removal was to be total. These items were not intended for ornamentation or even for sealing documents; they were to go into the treasury of the Lord.

The same principle was applied as Israel entered Canaan. It was specifically ordered at the conquest of Jericho, "All the silver, and gold, and vessels of brass and iron, are consecrated unto the Lord: they shall come into the treasury of the Lord" (Josh. 6:19). Achan violated that order, and his family died as a penalty for the disobedience.

Rings and Kings

With one possible exception, there is no record that any of the kings of Israel or Judah ever used a signet ring in official business. That exception was Ahab. His wife Jezebel, daughter of King Ethbaal from a section of Assyria, brought into Israel all manner of pagan practices. When Ahab could not buy the property of Naboth, Jezebel had a sinister plan to obtain it. "She wrote letters in Ahab's name, and sealed them with his seal" (I Kings 21:8). Thereby she secured the death of Naboth, and got the vineyard for her husband. It is not surprising that such a woman, who introduced Baal worship and the painted face into Israel, might also persuade her husband to utilize a signet ring. This is not certain, however. The word used for "seal" is the same as that translated "signet" in other places, but there were some seals that were not signet rings. Even if it was a signet, it was probably a cylinder rather than a finger ring, as cylinders were the custom in Assyria, from which Jezebel came.

There are frequent references to writings by other kings, but not one allusion to a ring being used to express authority. The signet originated where writing was not well known. But writing was common in Israel, and the kings practiced it.

Pen and Ink

The Lord spoke unto Isaiah and said, "Take thee a great roll, and write in it with a man's pen concerning Maher-shalal-hash-baz. And I took unto me faithful witnesses to record, Uriah the priest, and Zechariah" (Isa. 8:1, 2). Instead of a signet certifying genuineness, witnesses did so.

It was Baruch who wrote for Jeremiah. When asked how he did all that writing, he replied, "He pronounced all these words unto me with his mouth, and I wrote them with ink in the book" (Jer. 36:18).

That even children were taught to write is shown in Isaiah 10:19, "And the rest of the trees of his forest shall be few, that a child may write them."

The Subscription of Witnesses

To assure a return to the Holy Land, God told Jeremiah to buy some land from his cousin. Jeremiah relates it: "And gave the evidence of the purchase unto Baruch . . . in the sight of Hanameel mine uncle's son, and in the presence of the witnesses that subscribed the book of the purchase, before all the Jews that sat in the court of the prison" (Jer. 32:12). Witnesses subscribed, or signed, the document to show that it was genuine. Then it was all sealed up, or closed, and put away in an earthen vessel, so that it would last until it was needed again.

Though silence does not constitute proof, it appears that signet rings were never used to establish authority in Israel, unless it may have been done by wicked Ahab.

Pagan Practices With Rings

For Adornment

A trend from mere utility to showy adornment was explained in the last discussion. Although adornment is the primary function today, there may be some places where utility is still dominant. Britannica relates, "Among the Battas of Sumatra rings of a certain form are used to this day as passports."

Starting among kings, men of wealth and power, rings soon took on the evidence of affluence as well as of authority. The wearing of them moved beyond the circle of kings to others of means, who desired to show their class distinction by their adornment. One such man is referred to in James 2:2, "A man with a gold ring, in goodly apparel."

Aristotle, that renowned master of ancient philosophy, wore many rings upon his hand. His teacher, Plato, objected to such showiness, and it has been stated that this was a chief cause of the dissension that arose between them. Aristotle evidently felt that his teaching would be enhanced by such a display of wealth.

Kunz has commented, "The wearing of rings as ornaments for the hand requires no explanation in view of the innate love of adornment shown from the very earliest periods of human history. . . .

"The externals of luxurious adornment made, perhaps, a more direct appeal than the mere power of logical exposition could do, and such an eminently practical thinker as Aristotle was may not have been blind to these considerations" (Kunz, *Rings for the Finger*).

For More Adornment

Once the trend toward showiness is released from restraint, it is amazing to what lengths it will go. A whole book could be written on the subject, but a few illustrations must suffice. One ring seen in a French museum was made of gold with an extravagant bezel, or raised portion. It had a helmet and shield of sapphire, and a coat of arms was placed on the shield. Supporting the shield were a swan made of white chalcedony, and a bear made of emerald.

An Italian ring which became rather popular had baskets and nosegays of flowers, the flowers being made of gems and pearls, while the stems and leaves were of gold.

The French writer Bachaument has related how the number and size of rings increased in the 18th century. A sale was held in 1784, at which "200 rings rivaling one another in magnificence" were sold from the possessions of a single lady. Another writer recorded, "when one takes the hand of a pretty woman, one only has the sensation of holding a quantity of rings and angular stones, and it would be necessary first to strip these off the hand before we could perceive its form and delicacy" *(Ibid.)*.

A Vial of Poison

In Medieval Europe a special kind of ring was sometimes used to bring death, either to an enemy or to the wearer. One type had a sliding panel beneath the bezel, and in the tiny compartment thus concealed could be placed a vial of poison. Rather than to face an ignominious death in battle, a warrior might take the poison and end his own life. The noted leader Hannibal wore such a ring, since he was determined not to be captured by his rivals, the Romans.

In one of the robberies which brought Crassus such great wealth, he took the gold from a temple treasury. The temple guard, rather than face the consequences of that loss, seized his ring between his teeth, crushed the stone and sucked the poison from beneath it, thus bringing instant death to himself. The noted Greek orator Demosthenes also carried such a ring.

Another type of poison ring was more subtle, and obviously for the purpose of bringing death to a second party. One example contained a lion carved on the bezel, with hollow claws connected to a vial of poison hidden beneath. When pressure was exerted on the bezel, a mechanical trigger forced the liquid out through the lion's claws, much like a snake's bite forces poison into the victim. On some occasions the wearer would turn the bezel inward, so that as he shook hands with an enemy he could force poison into his veins. Surely Judas wasn't the last person who disguised treachery under a friendly gesture!

Perfume Vials

A less diabolical design than the above was involved in a perfume ring. It had a hidden compartment like the former, but it was used to contain a perfume instead of a poison. With a slight pressure on the ring, a subtle spray of perfume could be released into the atmosphere. Sometimes a disinfectant was used in an effort to combat ill health or foulness in the air.

Promise of Healing

Fantastic prescriptions for cures through use of rings were made by even medical practitioners in Roman society. A finger ring made of a rhinoceros' hoof would cure nervous problems and nightmares. Weak or sore eyes could be improved by use of a ring that had been placed in a glass with a blind lizard. A ring of jacinth protected travelers from danger or pestilence and assured them good sleep. Sapphire removed impurities from the eyes and cured carbuncles.

At a time when Catholic nuns were forbidden to wear rings with precious stones, an exception was made for some of them in 1263, in case of illness. Even churchmen were persuaded of ring power over disease!

There are many more uses to which rings have been put, and some of them will be discussed later.

Why Rings Were Worn

The Finger Watch

Some reasons have already been given why the wearing of finger rings was so popular in ancient times. The first ones were signets, followed by more and more elaborate ones for decorative purposes. An interesting form used in the 18th century was the sundial ring. Around the flat bezel were the names of months. A movable ring lay on the bezel inside the month names. It could be moved one way or the other to agree with the month of the year in which the time was to be determined. Inside this movable ring were the hours of the day. When the ring was held up in the sunlight, a ray of light passed through a tiny hole in the movable portion and fell on the proper hour of the day. A person, of course, had to know the direction of true north in order to get an accurate reading.

Some rings to indicate time were set with pearls to make them more exquisite. There we have the forerunner of the modern wristwatch!

Memorial Rings

About the same time it became customary for persons of wealth or fame to leave behind them at their death a number of rings designated to be received by friends. Some of these were pledges that a portion of the estate would be given to the same persons; at later times they were largely sentimental in significance.

Richard the Second of England (1366-1400) stated in his will that nine rings were to be left to his close friends, five bishops and four nobles. Shakespeare wrote his will on March 25, 1616, and specified that from his possessions money was to be spent for rings to be given to four fellowcitizens and three actors in his great dramas. In current coin the price of each was about $3.00!

An event which popularized such rings was the death of Charles the First on the scaffold. His loyalist followers called it a martyrdom, and they fashioned many rings with the king's portrait on them, so they could be often reminded of their cause and thereby make open commitment to it.

An ornate form of the memorial was common in the 17th century. The bezel was a coffin, and it was upheld by two skeletons, one on either side and bent along the band of the ring. These were commonly enameled in black and white, and bore the name and date of death of the departed person. Another common form had a lock of the departed person's hair set in the bezel, sometimes without form, but more frequently formed like a tree or some other design.

Connections With Spirits and Magic

Already it has been related that the first finger rings came into being because Jupiter forced Prometheus to wear on his finger a link of chain with a piece of the rock to which he had been sentenced to be chained for life; this according to an ancient Greek fable.

Another explanation of its origin says that the first ring was a knotted cord or wire worn as a charm. The knot signified the binding of a spell over the designated person, either the wearer or another. If over the wearer, the spell was for protection against any evil spirit that might cause lameness or disease. Again, the spell might be cast over an enemy, in order that he should lose the use of his faculties or members of his body.

From this beginning there has been a long history of magical connections with rings and their wearers. Some of them are utterly fantastic. Here is a sample—the tale of Solomon's ring.

An Arab legend asserted that all of Solomon's power and success came from an inherent quality in his ring. Ability which the Bible clearly attributes to God was thus taken from Him and given to a mere ring! The legend went on to declare that for forty years Solomon lost his power because he took off his ring while bathing, and an evil spirit carried it away. After the forty years, he found it again in a fish that was served at his table.

To the legend certain rabbis added that an extremely precious stone in the ring served as a magic mirror in which Solomon could see reflected any person or place about which he needed information.

Still another version had it that Solomon fell in love with a Gentile beauty, a prisoner named Aminah, and gave to her his ring. An evil spirit stole it from her, assumed Solomon's form, and became king, while making Solomon so ugly that his own people deposed him. One of Solomon's ministers recognized the evil spirit, however, and overcame him by reciting some verses from the Law. The evil spirit fled and dropped the ring into the sea, where it was devoured by a fish. Solomon, now working for a fisherman, found the ring and returned to his throne.

Superstition

One example must suffice here. In the pre-Christian era it was commonly believed that rings had the power of foretelling the future. If a number of signets were thrown into a pile and one drawn out at random, its engraving was a certain omen of things to come. Plutarch wrote, for example, of a battle under the Greek general Timoleon who was fighting to liberate Syracuse. Utterly confounded as to how to proceed, he gathered the rings from his men, drew one out of the collection, and by its wisdom swept to an overwhelming victory.

So from a very early time rings were assigned the attributes of wisdom, power, and guidance, which pertain to God alone.

The Magic Fascination of the Ring

Formula for Success

An old papyrus of the third century contains a formula for making a magic ring. Written in Greek and Egyptian, it assured a "ring to obtain (a wish) a favor and success; it renders glorious, great, admirable, and rich; it insures love. It is proper and excellent to be worn on all occasions, this incomparable ring. It bears the wonderful name of the sun . . . and is fashioned as follows: A complete serpent, like a circle, holding its tail in its mouth; on the inside is a scarab, sacred and radiant. As to the name, thou shalt engrave this in sacred characters on the reverse side of the gem, as is taught by the prophets, and thou shalt wear the ring in all purity. Having it with thee, all thy wishes will be fulfilled; the hatred of kings and emperors toward thee will be appeased; when thou wearest it all that thou sayest to others will be believed, all will favor thee, all doors will be open to thee. Thou wilt rend the bonds and break the stone walls, if thou takest out the stone, that is the gem, and pronouncest the name inscribed beneath it. This ring is equally useful for demoniacs. Give it to them, and on the instant the demon will flee" (Kunz, *Rings for the Finger*).

Plainly the ring was a substitute for God himself! Even He does not give unqualified promises so all-embracing!

Casting Out Demons

Josephus, the Jewish historian, told of a magic ring that had the power to exorcise demon spirits. Eleazar, a Jew, demonstrated its ability in the presence of Vespasian the emperor, his entire court, and his son. A number of persons supposedly suffering from demon possession were brought before him for treatment. Eleazar's ring had a portion of a special herb beneath the bezel, and when the ring was placed in the nose of the patient, the demon was attracted to it, leaving the body of the possessed one. Eleazar then recited some "Psalms of Solomon" as a chant, and ordered the demon to forsake the victim. (The herb was also prescribed by Solomon, he said.) In order to assure the watchers that the demon was real, Eleazar commanded it to upset a vase of water sitting on the ground, and reportedly it did so (Josephus, *Antiquities of the Jews,* Book VIII, Chap. 2).

In certain countries even today, Egypt for example, there is an awesome regard for the Evil Eye, a sinister influence possessed by certain people who can by their mere glance work destruction upon those whom they see, according to the superstition. The belief goes back to at least five centuries B.C. From that time there still exist rings which were used to combat the malevolent force of the Evil Eye. One such ring is of bronze with an amethyst set engraved as a human eye, which should overcome the evil one.

A Roman ring of the third century A.D. was used for the same purpose. Its entire bezel was an eye, and the entire ring weighed over two ounces.

Love and Lust

As a variant of memorial rings, worn to honor the dead, there were often rings worn with portraits and names of living persons who were greatly loved or admired. A stone could be lifted from the bezel to reveal the hidden portrait.

The supporters of Napoleon hoped, even after his exile to Elba, that he would return to France and be restored as emperor. To keep their hope alive, they wore rings with his picture done in enamel. A casket of gold could be opened on the ring, and the picture seen within it. Followers who shared the hope of his return were thus identified one to another, and encouraged to keep hoping for his restoration to power.

For love and admiration, lust was sometimes substituted. Xerxes, the Persian king, is said to have worn a signet adorned with the nude figure of Anahita, the Persian goddess of fertilization and also of war.

Self-Worship

In Egypt during Bible times, a special form of signet was often worn by the kings, who wished to exalt themselves to the level of a god. King Thothmes II gave to his queen a ring engraved from exquisite stone, with the words, "Flesh and blood of Amen Ra" (principal deity of ancient Egypt), thus indicating his opinion that he was the True One. His successor had an even bolder claim to deity: "Beautiful God, Conqueror of All Lands." Also on the stone was an engraved figure of a man-headed lion crushing a fallen foe beneath his foot.

These summaries reveal to what appalling extent the wearing of rings in ancient days was connected with superstition, fortune telling, lust, and even blasphemy. Surely it was a mark of paganism!

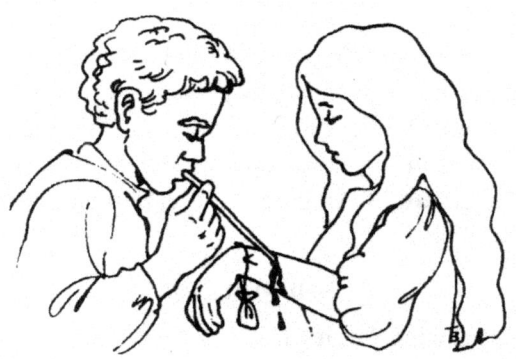

Rings of Love and Betrothal

A Token of Love

Among the many purposes for which rings have sometimes been worn, expression of love is one of them. The last study related how the wearing of a ring could be used to keep loyalty to a beloved leader alive and strong. Not only love of a follower for a leader could be shown in this way though; courting lovers, or even those who aspired to be such, might wear rings as tokens of their love for an absent one.

When either a lady or gentleman wanted to express love to a possible sweetheart, a ring was often given for the purpose. The Roman poet Ovid wrote of such as "a ring soon destined to encircle the finger of a beauteous girl, a ring having no worth except the love of the giver" (quoted by Kunz, *Rings for the Finger*).

Betrothal rings were common for a considerable time before wedding rings appeared. *Britannica* asserts that betrothal rings were an old Roman custom, and that the development from them to wedding rings can no longer be traced. Kunz says that the custom of such betrothal rings goes back to the second century B.C., and that plain iron rings were used for the purpose. It was only after some 400 years that gold ones appeared, and then often only for public display, the iron ones being worn at home.

The first occurrence of wedding rings was simply the use of the betrothal rings, which had been given earlier as tokens of fidelity. Along with them was often given a key or a signet. indicating that the spouse was entitled to all the property of her fiance.

The Blood Covenant

That is the title of a book by H. Clay Trumbull, published in 1885, in which he traced the betrothal ring back to the custom of entering a blood covenant with a friend. In this ancient ritual two persons had a vein opened in arm or hand, and each partook of some of the blood of the other. A pledge was written of absolute faithfulness each to the other even to death, and each enclosed a copy in a small leather pouch. which was suspended by a string around the arm or neck. From such a bracelet or necklace came the practice of a betrothal bracelet, in which two persons entered a covenant of love. The practice was of pagan origin, he asserted, and it is probable that the betrothal and wedding rings were evolved from that practice.

Trumbull gave an interesting evidence of the pagan origin of rings: "In South Australia, the rite of circumcision is one of the steps by which a lad enters into the sphere of manhood. This involves his covenanting with his new godfather, and with his new fellows in the sphere of his entering. In this ceremony, the very ring of flesh itself is placed 'on the third finger of the boy's left hand. . . .' What clearer indication than this is needed, that the finger-ring is a vestige of the primitive blood-covenant token?"

Desire for Union With God

Trumbull insisted that all blood covenanting originated from an innate desire for union with God. "From the beginning, and everywhere, blood seems to have been looked upon as preeminently the representative of life; as, indeed, in a peculiar sense, life itself. The transference of blood from one organism to another has been counted the transference of life, with all that life includes. The inter-commingling of blood by its inter-transference has been understood as equivalent to an inter-commingling of natures. Two natures thus inter-commingled . . . have been considered as forming, thenceforward, one blood, one life, one nature, one soul in two organisms. . . .

"A covenant of blood, a covenant made by the intercommingling of blood, has been recognized as the closest, the holiest, and the most indissoluble, compact conceivable. Such a covenant clearly involves an absolute surrender of one's separate self, and an irrevocable merging of one's individual nature into the dual, or the multiplied, personality included in the compact. Man's highest and noblest outreachings of soul have, therefore, been of such a union with the divine nature as is typified in this human covenant of blood" *(Ibid.)*.

"Among all peoples, from the beginning, sacrifice has been a means of seeking union with the divine—with God or with the gods. And through sacrifice this divine-human interunion has been deemed a possibility, in all lands and always. The idea of such a union between the human nature and the divine has inevitably come to partake of the grossness of the religious conceptions of the different people holding it; but even in its grossest form it has remained a witness to the primal truth which prompted it" *(Ibid.)*.

Summary

The foregoing are extremely significant words. In brief they assert that from the beginning all people have had an innate desire for the life of God. But cut off from Him through sin, and not knowing how to find His life, they have substituted the lifeblood of a substitute, and in mingling their own blood with that of another have felt that in some way they were coming into union with Him.

As will be made plain in the next study, the betrothal and wedding rings are remnants of one form of covenant designed to bring about such a union of blood.

Origin of the Wedding Ring

More From *The Blood Covenant*

Extensive quotation was made from Trumbull's book in the previous study. Even longer quotations are given here, because of the great significance it has concerning the origin of the wedding ring. At first betrothal rings were used at the wedding, but later a separate ring was introduced. In either case the origin is the same.

"It would, indeed, seem that from this root-idea of the binding force of an endless covenant, symbolized in the form, and in the primitive name, of the bracelet, the armlet, the ring—there has come down to us the use of the wedding-ring, or the wedding-bracelet. . . .

"The use of rings, or bracelets. or armlets, in the covenant of betrothal, or of marriage, is from of old, and it is of widespread acceptance. References to it are cited from Pliny, Tertullian, Juvenal, Isidore; and traces of it are found, earlier or later, among the people of Asia. Africa, Europe, and the Island of the Sea. In Iceland, the covenanting-ring was large enough for the palm of the hand to be passed through; so in betrothal 'the bridegroom passed four fingers and his palm through one of these rings, and in this manner he received the hand of the bride.' "

Showing that some of the early wedding rings were worn on the thumb, Trumbull continued, "Chardin reports a form of marriage in Ceylon, by the binding together of the thumbs of the contracting parties; as, according to the classics, the thumbs were bound together in the rite of blood-covenanting. Indeed, the selection of the ring-finger for the wedding-covenant has commonly been attributed to the relation of that finger to the heart as the blood-centre, and as the seat of life" (Trumbull, T*he Blood Covenant*).

Ancient Practices

"Among the Copts of Egypt, both the blood and the ring have their part in the covenant of marriage. Two rings are employed, one for the bride and one for the bridegroom. At the door of the bridegroom's house, as the bride approaches it, a lamb or a sheep is slaughtered; and the bride must have a care to step over the covenanting blood as she enters the door, to join the bridegroom. It is after the ceremony, that the two contracting parties exchange the rings, which are as the tokens of the covenant of blood. . . .

"Again, in Little Russia, the bride gives to the bridegroom a covenanting draught in 'a cup of wine, in which a ring has been put'; as if in that case the wine and the blood-bond of the covenant were commingled" *(Ibid.).*

These illustrations are given to show that betrothal and wedding rings had their origin in the practice of blood-covenanting. That in turn came in response to an innate desire for oneness with God, as was shown in the former study. In support of this fact, here is a further word from Trumbull: "It is not improbable indeed, that the armlets, or bracelets, which were found on the arms of Oriental kings, and of Oriental divinities as well, were intended to indicate, or to symbolize, the personal inter-union claimed to exist between those kings and divinities. Thus an armlet worn by Thothmes III is preserved in the museum at Leyden. It bears the symbol of the King, having on it his sacred name, with its reference to his inter-union with his god. It was much the same in Nineveh."

Practices of the Pagans

As the Coptic practice illustrates, there is a connection between the ancient, prevalent rite of blood covenanting and the form of blood sacrifice which God established for His people after Adam's sin. Those Coptics didn't originate the slaughter of the lamb; God did. Although they much distorted and misapplied the sacrifice, they felt the need for bloodshed and a covenant bond, which Trumbull has shown is based on desire for union with God.

The wedding ring, placed on the fourth finger, which supposedly has a vein directly connected with the heart, is thus one of the symbols from paganism derived from a distorted view about the way to find the life of God. Those pagans believed that life was in the blood; that since we can't get blood from God, we must get it from a substitute—animal or person; that a blood covenant with any person is thus a way to find the life of God; that a marriage covenant is one such way to God's life; that the fourth finger has a connection with blood direct from the heart; and that therefore a ring on that finger symbolizes an endless covenant which in some way substitutes for the life of God which has been so far lost.

Not every person involved with the wedding ring thought that all out clearly. However the pattern is now traced, and we see what the ring symbolized: a search for God among those who didn't know how to find Him otherwise.

We now know the way to God, through His blessed Son, our Saviour, and that symbolism is no longer needed.

The Use of Symbols

Review

Betrothal rings, and later wedding rings, were shown by H. Clay Trumbull to have evidently originated from the prevalent practice of blood covenanting. That in turn came from an innate desire in men's hearts to find fellowship with God and to share His life. Through Adam's fall and the heathen darkness which then descended over the earth, the way to God was obscured. In the darkness there arose a multitude of ceremonies and symbols which gave evidence that there still existed in the human heart a need for Him and a desire to find Him.

The Distortion of Symbols

Trumbull explained how the common symbols of paganism got their start. For people who believe that God created a perfect world, which later fell into sin and darkness, the explanation is quite clear: a common revelation from God was given to men in the beginning; all of the signs of religious striving are just the perverted remnants of that rejected revelation.

Kurtz, in his *History of the Old Covenant* (Vol. 1), said, "The symbols which were transferred from the religions of nature to that of the spirit, first passed through the fire of divine purification, from which they issued as the distinctive theology of the Jews; the dross of a pantheistic deification of nature having been consumed. . . . Every error, however dangerous, is based on some truth misunderstood, and . . . every aberration, however grievous, has started from a desire after real good, which had not attained its goal, because the latter was sought neither in the right way, nor by the right means" (quoted by Trumbull, *The Blood Covenant*).

The conclusion is quite clear: since the symbols arose through pagan gropings after God, and since the way to Him is now open and plain, the pagan symbols are no longer necessary.

Other Views of Symbolism

Trumbull's observations are not the only possible explanation of the ring's beginning. An old book, *How the World Weds*, by Claudia De Lys, explained that when a caveman found a prospective wife, he bound her about the wrists and ankles with ropes of grasses and rushes, so she would not depart from him. As she learned his power and became accustomed to his authority, she could be retained with ropes only around the wrists, and then finally with only a ring of rushes around one finger.

Paul Berdanier wrote a somewhat similar view in his book, *How It Began*. He said, "Our earliest ancestors thought a rope tied around part of the body would keep the soul from escaping. When a man captured his mate, he tied cords around her waist, wrists, and ankles to make sure her spirit was held under his control. Later a permanent ring of ivory, flint, or amber took the place of the rope to symbolize obedience of the wearer to a higher power" (both quotes from James R. McCarthy, *Rings Through the Ages*, p. 154). The ancient Pharaohs of Egypt, according to McCarthy, were the first to draw the circle as a heavenly sign of life, love, and happiness, since the circle like eternity has no beginning and no ending.

Tubal-Cain, the Metal Smith

Genesis 4:22 says, "And Zillah, she also bare Tubal-Cain, an instructor of every artificer in brass and iron." Tubal-Cain was a sixth-generation descendant of Cain, and thus perhaps a contemporary of Enoch. Here is a tradition about him and the wedding ring:

> In an old Latin work, ascribing the invention of the ring to Tubal-Cain, we find, "The form of the ring being circular, that is, round, and without end, importeth thus much, that mutual love and hearty affection should roundly flow from one to the other, as a circle, and that continually and for ever...."
>
> However, like everything, humanly speaking, the wedding ring has had its vicissitudes, and from being the emblem of all that is pure and holy in life, has been desecrated to the vilest and most impious of usages (quoted in William Jones, *Finger-Ring Lore*, pp. 276, 282).

The ascription of the ring to Tubal-Cain, however, seems to be fanciful, perhaps because he was a metal smith. The degradation of the ring involved the show of decency in clandestine marriages, plus other fraudulent uses.

A Change of Symbolism

In due time the Roman Catholic Church accepted and blessed the use of the ring in marriages. *Britannica* says, "The giving of a ring to mark a betrothal was an old Roman custom.... This use of the ring, which was thus of purely secular origin, received ecclesiastical sanction, and formulae of benediction of the ring exist from the 11th century. The exact stages by which the wedding ring developed from the betrothal ring can no longer be traced." Kunz asserted that the change first appeared in England about the time of the Reformation. Earlier than that, while the betrothal ring was still used for the wedding, a new meaning was given to it within the Roman church. Bishop Durant, who died in 1296, said that for him it was a symbol of mutual love between those espoused to each other, and a pledge that their hearts were to be united together (Kunz, *Rings for the Finger*).

God's Jewels

His Choice of Symbols

Before a return to specific treatment of rings, let there be some discussion about the general subject of jewelry in the Bible. Much clamor is heard for the wearing of jewelry because of what it is taken to symbolize. It is good to recall, though, that God himself has established some rich symbols in the Bible which involve jewels. Before turning away from the symbolism He has established, a person should consider seriously whether it is justified or not.

All of the following symbols are derived from the *value* which jewels have. (Gold and silver may be treated in the same category.) They were the most valuable items known in the material realm in Bible times. And even today there are very few natural objects which surpass them in price. Such value depends on four qualities: beauty, serviceability, purity, and durability.

The Beauty of God's Character

Precious metals and precious stones symbolize the beauty of God's holy character! One cannot mistake this fact in reading about preparations that were made for both the Tabernacle and the Temple. Prescriptions for the priestly garments, as well as for the house, involved such exquisite beauty. "Thou shalt make holy garments for Aaron thy brother for glory and for beauty" (Ex. 28:2). Following instructions specify the kinds of precious stones to be placed on the breastplate and upon the ephod; the gold plating to cover the furnishings of the tabernacle; and the engraving on the plate to be worn on the priest's forehead, HOLINESS UNTO THE LORD (28:36).

Much more elaborate was the prescription for gold and precious stones to beautify the Temple. The Lord himself showed David the exact pattern for the Temple, which was committed to Solomon to build. That pattern included indescribable beauty that awed David greatly. I Chronicles, Chapters 28 and 29, are most impressive in their detailed catalog of exquisite jewels, some of which David had already provided, and some of which the people were asked to supply.

Here is a little part of David's speech: "The palace is not for man, but for the Lord God. Now I have prepared with all my might for the house of my God the gold for things to be made of gold . . . onyx stones, and stones to be set, glistering stones, and of divers colours, and all manner of precious stones, and marble stones in abundance. . . . And they with whom precious stones were found gave them to the treasure of the house of the Lord. . . . Then the people rejoiced, for that they offered willingly, because with perfect heart they offered willingly to the Lord: and David the king also rejoiced with great joy."

The Glitter, the Gold, and the Glory

II Chronicles 3:5 continued the story as Solomon constructed the house of the Lord: "And the greater house he ceiled with fir tree, which he overlaid with fine gold, and set thereon palm trees and chains. And he garnished the house with precious stones for beauty: and the gold was gold of Parvaim. He overlaid also the house, the beams, the posts, and the walls thereof, and the doors thereof, with gold; and graved cherubims on the walls.

... And the weight of the nails was fifty shekels of gold. And he overlaid the upper chambers with gold."

On and on the story goes: more and more gold, glistering stones, beauty—glory—holiness! This was God's house!

The nails weighed fifty shekels. That is twenty ounces, and at recent price of gold was worth more than $5,000! What nails they were!

Adam Clarke estimated the total value of gold and silver in the Temple, and at the exchange rate before current inflation the figure was over six billion dollars. That did not include the precious stones! Imagine the impressiveness of walls, chains, doors, posts, beams, altars, and more, overlaid with the finest gold. And then visualize the garnishing of it all with inset stones of every rainbow color, sparkling from the light of golden candlesticks.

This was not for beautifying of somebody's flesh. No, it was God's chosen symbol to present His holiness, His beauty, His glory!

Serviceability

These treasures were not only beautiful, but serviceable. Diamonds are useful as tips for drills or phonograph needles. Gold and silver have qualities that qualify for valuable service. So it is with other stones and metals: they have a place to serve.

Gold and silver are malleable; they can be beaten into shape without breaking down. Silver can be drawn into a wire only one four-thousandth of an inch thick. At that rate one ounce could reach for twenty-five miles or more.

Describing Aaron's garments, Exodus 39:3-7 says, "They did beat the gold into thin plates, and cut it into wires, to work it in the blue, and in the purple, and in the scarlet, and in the fine linen, with cunning work. . . . And they wrought onyx stones inclosed in ouches of gold, graven, as signets are graven, with the names of the children of Israel. And he put them on the shoulders of the ephod, that they should be stones for a memorial to the children of Israel; as the Lord commanded Moses."

Can you and I be shaped as gold to serve the Lord?

The Symbol of Purity

The Pure and the Purified

Precious stones and precious metals signify the purity of God. Only in Him is there underived, spotless purity. Being pure by nature, God longs for His creatures to be pure as well, and He designs to purify them. Nothing less can satisfy His saving purpose.

Jewels were formed in the fire. Sometime in the distant past, when the earth was in formation, the cooling of molten material allowed those stones to crystallize in pure form. The lapidary never has to melt a diamond to make it pure. It already is so from its beginning. So is God pure, forever so, without any adulteration.

Gold must be separated from its ore and purified by fire. Silver is the same. These metals symbolize the process by which God brings His people to a purity like His own. Malachi 3:3 declares, "He shall sit as a refiner and purifier of silver: and he shall purify the sons of Levi, and purge them as gold and silver, that they may offer unto the Lord an offering in righteousness."

The Process of Refinement

There is a crisis of refinement, and there is a process by which it continues. "When he hath tried me, I shall come forth as gold," said Job in his time of suffering (23:10). Precious stones may be pure, but need polishing. So the lapidary works with care to bring from the "diamond in the rough" the finest possible jewel.

Even Jesus, the spotless Son of God, the brightest Jewel of heaven, was subjected to shaping and polishing on earth. "Though he were a Son, yet learned he obedience by the things which he suffered; and being made perfect, he became the author of eternal salvation unto all them that obey him" (Heb. 5:8, 9).

From among the foulest of earth, God's refinings can bring forth beauty and purity fit for the Bride of Christ. The Psalmist sang of it in Psalm 45:9, 13: "Kings' daughters were among thy honourable women: upon thy right hand did stand the queen in gold of Ophir. . . . The king's daughter is all glorious within: her clothing is of wrought gold." It is the inner character that is symbolized by such figures. As *Pulpit Commentary* says about the latter verse, "She is 'glorious,' not only without, in her robe of 'gold of Ophir,' but also and especially within—in the inner chamber of the heart—where she is indeed 'glorious,' through the sanctifying presence of God's Holy Spirit."

The Heavenly Jeweler

With what eagerness does our Lord wait the day when His bride shall be presented to Him! Speaking of a day when the proud are happy, wicked men are exalted, and God's tempters appear safe, Malachi said, "Then they that feared the Lord spake often one to another. . . . And they shall be mine, saith the Lord of hosts, in that day when I make up my jewels" (3:16, 17). Jewels represent people, those who have been refined and who endure faithfully under scorn and rejection of men.

When people sacrifice their purity for popularity—when the jewel quality is lost—judgment is not far away. Jeremiah lamented (and doubtless God did also), "How is the gold become dim! how is the most fine gold changed! the stones of the sanctuary are poured out in the top of every street. The precious sons of Zion, comparable to fine gold, how are they esteemed as earthen pitchers, the work of the hands of the potter! . . . Her Nazarites were purer than snow . . . they were more ruddy in body than rubies, their polishing was of sapphire: their visage is blacker than a coal. . . . The Lord hath accomplished his fury" (Lam. 4:1, 2, 7, 8, 11).

The world seeks after jewels for the flesh; God seeks for jewels of the spirit. He put the gems here as symbols of what is pure in His sight.

Durability

The fourth source of a gem's value is its durability. Other things decay or wear out, but jewels keep on shining. They symbolize eternity.

It is not by accident that precious stones are found at both the beginning and the ending of the Bible. Genesis 2:12 describes the Eden of God, "And the gold of that land is good: there is bdellium and the onyx stone." Revelation 21 describes the New Jerusalem as having light like a jasper stone, walls of jasper, foundations garnished with all manner of precious stones, gates of pearl, and streets of pure gold. None shall ever defile it, but the saved shall freely enter. This is the place where the Bride dwells with the Bridegroom.

The stones of Eden pointed to eternity past. Those in the New Eden point to eternity future. They symbolize the things that endure when all else is shaken and broken down.

Wisdom is one: "There is gold, and a multitude of rubies: but the lips of knowledge are a precious jewel" (Prov. 20:15). "Wisdom is better than rubies" (Prov. 8:11).

The righteousness of the redeemed is another: "He hath clothed me with the garments of salvation, he hath covered me with the robe of righteousness, as a bridegroom decketh himself with ornaments, and as a bride adorneth herself with her jewels" (Isa. 61:10). This is not a recommendation of earthly jewelry; it rather shows that jewels are chosen of God to represent spiritual realities. Should we not keep to His symbolism?

Works with eternal value are yet another: "Now if any man build upon this foundation gold, silver, precious stones . . . the fire shall try every man's work of what sort it is. If any man's work abide which he hath built thereupon, he shall receive a reward"(I Cor. 3:12-14). Are we building for eternity, or just for time?

The Misuse of Jewelry

Lifted Up Because of Beauty

A brief summary of the Bible record will reveal a number of incidents concerning the misuse of jewelry. As has already been seen, God designed precious stones and metals as symbols of His own character. Misuse of those things is often condemned in God's Word.

It is possible that the first transgression was with Satan himself. Commentators are not fully agreed, but from the time of the Early Church fathers a common interpretation of Ezekiel 28, declares that the king of Tyrus was a type of Lucifer who fell from heaven. (A parallel account is found in Isaiah 14 concerning the king of Babylon.) Though this cannot be finally proven, it does appear to fit with other Bible passages concerning the fall of Satan from heaven.

Ezekiel 28:12-17 says, in part, "Thou sealest up the sum, full of wisdom, and perfect in beauty. Thou hast been in Eden the garden of God; every precious stone was thy covering, the sardius, topaz, and the diamond, the beryl, the onyx, and the jasper, the sapphire, the emerald, and the carbuncle, and gold. . . . Thou wast upon the holy mountain of God; thou hast walked up and down in the midst of the stones of fire. Thou wast perfect in thy ways from the day that thou wast created, till iniquity was found in thee. . . . Thou hast sinned: therefore I will cast thee as profane out of the mountain of God: and I will destroy thee, O covering cherub, from the midst of the stones of fire. Thine heart was lifted up because of thy beauty, thou hast corrupted thy wisdom by reason of thy brightness: I will cast thee to the ground."

The Fall of Lucifer

Among those who see in the kings of Babylon and Tyre a figure of Satan's fall is G. H. Pember, who gave a lengthy explanation of it in his book, *Earth's Earliest Ages*. He pointed out the fact that Eden was God's dwelling place, with its three parts—Eden, the Garden, and the Mountain of God—being analogous to the tabernacle with its court, its holy place, and its holy of holies. In that holiest Lucifer dwelt before his fall, as a cherub guarding the presence of God.

God's dwelling place is always marked by the glory of precious stones. Moses and Aaron went up in the mountain of Sinai, "and they saw the God of Israel: and there was under his feet as it were a paved work of a sapphire stone, and as it were the body of heaven in his clearness. . . . And the sight of the glory of the Lord was like devouring fire on the top of the mount in the eyes of the children of Israel" (Ex. 24:10, 17). Associated with that glory was the appearance of flashing sapphire stones.

Placed in such a bright and beautiful spot, designed to reflect God's majesty, Lucifer envied the brightness and plotted that it should reflect his own brightness instead of God's. So those stones of fire—those radiant gems—were part of the occasion of his fall. He determined they should beautify himself instead of symbolizing God's glorious holiness. Thus he fell!

"How art thou fallen from heaven, O Lucifer, son of the morning! how art thou cut down to the ground, which didst weaken the nations! For thou hast said in thine heart, I will ascend into heaven . . . I will be like the most High. Yet thou shalt be brought down to hell, to the sides of the pit (Isa. 14:12-15).

Should not a mere man or woman think most seriously before following the course of Lucifer, putting God's jewels in place to glorify the creature rather than the Creator?

Identification With Idolatry

Several Bible passages link the wearing of jewels directly with idolatry. If Satan did indeed fall in part through the misappropriation of God's jewels, it is not surprising that he should seek to have those two practices linked together, for both are then means of taking God's glory from Him and giving it to another.

Rebuking His people for their apostasy, God said, "I will visit upon her the days of Baalim, wherein she burned incense to them, and she decked herself with her earrings and her jewels, and she went after her lovers, and forgat me, saith the Lord" (Hosea 2:13).

There was also the case of Jacob returning to Bethel, who ordered his family to put away all uncleanness. "And they gave unto Jacob all the strange gods which were in their hand, and all their earrings which were in their ears; and Jacob hid them under the oak which was by Shechem" (Gen. 35:4). Other cases are reported in Exodus 32:2-4; Ezekiel 23:26-44; and Jeremiah 4:30.

A Mark of Fleshliness and Sensuality

As idolatry was often connected with illicit sex, so jewelry became associated with sensuality. God rebuked His fallen people thus: "Though thou clothest thyself with crimson, though thou deckest thee with ornaments of gold, though thou rentest thy face with painting, in vain shalt thou make thyself fair; thy lovers will despise thee, they will seek thy life" (Jer. 4:30).

"When they had slain their children to their idols, then they came the same day into my sanctuary to profane it. . . . Ye have sent for men to come from far, unto whom a messenger was sent; and, lo, they came: for whom thou didst wash thyself, paintedst thy eyes, and deckedst thyself with ornaments, and satest upon a stately bed. . . . Yet they went in unto her, as they go in unto a woman that playeth the harlot" (Ezek. 23:39-41, 44).

In a day yet to come, as foretold in Revelation 17:4, the harlot woman which rode upon the beast, was "arrayed in purple and scarlet colour, and decked with gold and precious stones and pearls, having a golden cup in her hand full of abominations and filthiness of her fornication."

There is much of symbolism here, of course; but that is precisely the point being made: in God's Book the putting of His jewels on the flesh is abusing the symbolism which He has designed. Who has the right to do that, when God has not authorized it?

God's View of Human Jewelry

Separation Demanded

Already there has been given the record of Jacob and his family returning to Beth-el, where God had met him at the beginning. He ordered all of the false gods and jewels together to be given up, and he buried them beneath an oak tree. They were out of order as he took his family back to that sacred place where heaven was opened and he entered God's house.

When Israel worshiped the golden calf before Sinai, they also wore the jewels they had brought out of Egypt. In correcting their wickedness the Lord demanded that the calf be ground to powder, and that the jewels be removed (Ex. 33:1-6).

One of Moses' last official acts was to direct the campaign against the Midianites at God's command. The prey of animals and slaves was to be partly given to the people who fought in the campaign. All the confiscated gold and jewels the warriors started to treat likewise, keeping the major portion for themselves. "We have therefore brought an oblation for the Lord, what every man hath gotten, of jewels of gold, chains, and bracelets, rings, earrings, and tablets, to make an atonement for our souls before the Lord. And Moses and Eleazar the priest took the gold of them, even all wrought jewels . . . (For the men of war had taken spoil, every man for himself)" (Num. 31:50-53). Once more the people were forbidden to take any of the treasures unto themselves, but to bring them all to the Tabernacle of the Lord.

Falling Into a Snare

At the fall of Jericho, Achan disobeyed the Lord and took some silver and gold for himself, as well as a Babylonish garment. The whole nation suffered defeat as a consequence, and Achan died for his disobedience. God had ordered that all the precious things be brought into His treasury.

When Gideon led Israel to victory over the Midianites, he humbly refused to be made a king. He did succumb to a desire for some of the spoil, however, and asked the warriors to give him the gems collected from the vanquished. "And the weight of the golden earrings that he requested was a thousand and seven hundred shekels of gold; beside ornaments. . . . And Gideon made an ephod thereof, and put it in his city, even in Ophrah: and all Israel went thither a whoring after it: which thing became a snare unto Gideon, and to his house" (Judges 8:26, 27).

Does the sacred record not make plain the danger when people begin to covet God's jewels for themselves, as items of worship, fleshly adornment, or sensual attraction?

Judgment Upon Judah

Isaiah's prophecy begins with the announcement of a wicked nation, a backslidden people, and an angry God. Judgment is on its way! In Chapters 2 and 3 the prophet begins his description of specifics which so "provoked the Holy One of Israel unto anger."

First there were the sins of the men: "They be replenished from the east, and are soothsayers like the Philistines, and they please themselves in the children of strangers. Their land also is full of silver and gold, neither is there any end of their treasures . . . their land also is full of idols; they worship the work of their own hands, that which their own fingers have made" (2:6-8). Their sin was idolatry, and God pledged to humble them in their arrogance. "In that day a man shall cast his idols of silver, and his idols of gold, which they made . . . to worship, to the moles and to the bats" (2:20).

Then he turned to the sins of the women: "The daughters of Zion are haughty, and walk with stretched forth necks and wanton eyes, walking and mincing as they go, and making a tinkling with their feet. . . . In that day the Lord will take away the bravery of their tinkling ornaments" (3:16-18). Then he listed the items, including chains around the necks, bracelets, earrings, and rings.

The men with their idolatry and the women with their jewelry were alike under judgment: "Thy men shall fall by the sword, and thy mighty in the war. And her gates shall lament and mourn; and she being desolate shall sit upon the ground" (3:25, 26).

An Early Church Problem

Through the captivity in Babylon, Israel was largely purified from idolatry; to this day the Jews are determinedly opposed to it. The problem of jewelry was not that easily disposed of. George Kunz was quoted earlier in this series to the effect that there appeared to be an innate love for jewelry—rings in particular—from the beginnings of human history. That basic desire is present in most cultures even to this day.

Even in the Early Church the problem was present. So the apostles Paul and Peter both warned that adornment should not be that involving gold or pearls or other costly array, but should rather be the inner beauty of a Christlike spirit (I Tim. 2:9, 10; I Peter 3:3, 4).

It would appear that such warnings are very much in order today.

Laws About Rings

Moral Restraint

Writers already quoted in this series have referred to the "innate love of adornment," "externals of luxury," and the "widely spread natural impulse" for decoration which have been the basis for wearing of rings in most of the world's nations. Entirely beyond Biblical or Christian considerations, many of the nations have endeavored to control that natural impulse by special laws.

Such enactments are called sumptuary laws, and are based on moral considerations, designed to regulate personal expenditures when they tend toward extravagance and luxury. "Indeed any strict sumptuary regulation always implies the existence of an undue degree of luxury in the usages that are subjected to legal restraint" (Kunz, *Rings for the Finger*).

Many illustrations could be given of such laws. A few must suffice. Interestingly, almost all such efforts have failed, and the laws have either been abolished or ignored.

Egypt and Greece

From the evidence available it appears that ring wearing began in Egypt with some form of signet. Research of this writer has not found any kind of law which the Egyptians enacted to control ring use. Doubtless because of this lack, use spread from royalty to commoners, and there was an astounding profusion of jewelry. It will be recalled that when Moses and the Israelites left, they "stripped the Egyptians" and carried away a great quantity of jewelry to be used in the tabernacle.

Archaeological evidences, abundant because of the dry climate, show that frequently several rings were worn on each hand. Mummies were buried with them. Some specimens have been found to weigh as much as five ounces.

Common people, who could not afford elaborate rings, nevertheless wore them made of silver, bronze, glass, or pottery colored brightly and glazed to a shiny finish.

Greece derived the practice from the Egyptians. At an early date a sumptuary law was passed in Sparta limiting signet rings to materials no more valuable than iron. Some city states had no such laws.

Etruscan and Roman Practice

Etruria was an ancient country in central Italy. Ring wearing moved to Rome by way of the Etruscans, it appears. These latter people inclined to extravagance in size and elaboration of the rings they wore.

The Romans inclined to limit themselves to more simplicity, and regulations soon arose for that purpose. Average citizens wore none more valuable than iron rings, while the slaves were not permitted any. For a time nobody was allowed to wear gold, the first waiver being permitted to the ambassadors, and then only while they were on public duty. Gradually pressure built up for leniency, and permission was granted to senators, consuls, horsemen, and chief statesmen in that order.

During the period of the empire, until nearly 500 A.D., those who were not born as free citizens could not wear gold unless they owned much property. Later permission was given freely to Roman soldiers and to all free men. Those made free during their lifetime were then permitted to wear silver rings. Slaves were allowed to wear iron rings only. Finally, during the rule of Justinian, all restrictions were set aside.

Roman Catholic Rules

Within the Roman setting the Catholic Church soon faced the issue of ring wearing. Since authority rested with the pope, it was his prerogative to make such decisions. Some writers indicate that he was the first to wear one.

Bishops of the church were long forbidden them. The first reference available to an authorized signet ring for bishops was in 511 A.D. Several years earlier, though, it appears that some of them were already wearing them. A letter from Archbishop Avit of Vienne to Bishop Apollinarius of Valencia reads as follows, in part: "The ring you have been kind enough to offer me should be made as follows: In the middle of a very thin iron hoop, representing two dolphins facing each other, a double seal should be made by means of two pivots, so that either side may be shown or hidden at will and in turn, and offer, alternately, to the eyes a green stone or a pale electrum. . . . Let my monogram be engraved on the seal surrounded by my name, so that it may be read" (Quoted in *Ibid.*). This was obviously not an official ring authorized by the pope.

In other countries where Romanism went, restrictions were often made which were not observed in Rome. As late as the early 20th century, a high representative of the Russian church declared that none of the clergy of the church wore rings of any kind. Their seals were not made in the form of signets.

Although some lay people of the church were wearing rings with Christian symbols at a much earlier date, the first permission for use of the wedding ring with ecclesiastical sanction and priestly benediction was about the 11th century. Considering that gold rings for weddings were already being used by Roman society in general from the 2nd century, it is rather amazing that the church stood against them for some 700 years!

The Ring in Church History

Words from Tertullian

There is no evidence that the Early Church placed its approval on ring wearing. Kunz stated, "Perhaps the earliest allusion in Christian literature to the betrothal ring appears in one of Tertullian's writings, dated from the end of the second century A.D., wherein he says: 'Among our women the time-honored rules of their ancestors, which enjoined modesty and sobriety, have died out. In former times women knew nothing of gold except the single betrothal ring . . .'" (Kunz, *Rings for the Finger*). Tertullian's expression "former times" seems to refer to pre-Christian days. His words make clear, though, that wearing of jewelry was becoming a real problem among the Christian women. Even within the pages of the New Testament, the writings of Paul and Peter indicate the same, as has already been noted. This inclination to increased wearing of gold indicated a death of modesty and sobriety, Tertullian said.

Clemens of Alexandria

Clemens lived from about 150 to 217 A.D. In his *Paedagogus* he said, "Although the Christian women of the early

Christian centuries were taught to avoid all superfluous adornments, the wearing of a gold ring was permitted to them. This was not, however, to be considered as an ornament, but was simply for use in sealing up the household goods entrusted to a wife's care. Nevertheless while noting this use, Clemens Alexandrinus . . . adds that if both servants and masters were properly instructed in their respective duties and obligations, there would be no need for such precautions" *(Ibid.).*

The ring to which Clemens referred was signet which was used as a seal. In his discourse entitled "The Instructor" he wrote more on the subject: "And if it is necessary for us, while engaged in public business. or discharging other avocations in the country, and often away from our wives, to seal anything for the sake of safety, He (the Word) allows us a signet for this purpose only. Other finger-rings are to be cast off, since according to the Scripture 'instruction is a golden ornament for a wise man' " *(The Ante-Nicene Fathers,* Vol. II).

Writing particularly of women, he asserted, "If one thinks himself made beautiful by gold, he is inferior to gold. . . . Those women that are luxurious to excess in their wantonness, elated by wealth, dishonour by the stains of amatory indulgences [sensual gratification] what is true beauty. . . .

"For women's articles of luxury are to be prohibited, as things of swift wing producing unstable follies and empty delights; by which, elated and furnished with wings, they often fly away from the marriage bond" *(Ibid.).* This church father thus recognized that the wearing of jewelry of any kind did not tend to perpetuate marriages, but rather to weaken or even destroy them.

The Bishop of Carthage

Early in the third century Cyprian was the bishop of Carthage in North Africa. In his "Treatises" he wrote strong words for young virgins, warning them against any corruption of their faith or virtue: "It is becoming for no Christian, and especially it is not becoming for a virgin, to regard any glory and honor of the flesh, but only to desire the Word of God, to embrace benefits which shall endure for ever. Or, if she must glory in the flesh, then assuredly let her glory when she is tortured in confession of the name; when a woman is found to be stronger than the tortures; when she suffers fire, or the cross, or the sword, or the wild beasts, that she may be crowned. These are the precious jewels of the flesh, these are better ornaments of the body....

"The characteristics of ornaments, and of garments, and the allurements of beauty, are not fitting for any but prostitutes and immodest women; and the dress of none is more precious than of those whose modesty is lowly. Thus in the Holy Scriptures, by which the Lord wished us to be both instructed and admonished, the harlot city is described more beautifully arrayed and adorned, and with her ornaments; and the rather on account of those very ornaments about to perish. . . . Let chaste and modest virgins avoid the dress of the unchaste, the manners of the immodest, the ensigns of brothels, the ornaments of harlots. . . .

"Be such as God the Creator made you. . . . Let your countenance remain in you incorrupt, your neck unadorned, your figure simple; let not wounds be made in your ears, nor let the precious chain of bracelets and necklaces circle your arms or your neck; let your feet be free from golden bands, your hair stained with no dye, your eyes worthy of beholding God. . . . Overcome dress, since you are a virgin; overcome gold, since you overcome the flesh and the world" *(Ibid.).*

It may be observed that Cyprian made no mention of the wedding ring. This is doubtless explained by two considerations. First, even in pagan Rome the wedding ring did not appear until in the second century A.D., and Cyprian wrote in Africa early in the third century—probably before the ring became a problem there. Second, he was writing to virgins, whose problem would not be the wedding ring, but other forms of adornment.

The Ring Rolls On

Futile Efforts

For several reasons there have been numerous historical efforts to prohibit the wearing of rings, as well as of other types of jewelry. Probably the first reason was the recognition that such items of apparel promote extravagance and excess, to which the natural impulses of the human heart easily fall prey. Pagan Rome, as has been observed, enacted laws to prohibit or to restrict ring wearing. In the Roman Catholic Church as well, for centuries there were laws which made similar restrictions. They proved ineffectual, however, and they were finally dropped.

A second reason for opposition to the ring was the belief that New Testament principles forbade it. Cyprian, for example, who was cited in the previous discussion, quoted Timothy 2:9, 10 and I Peter 3:3, 4, and followed by saying, "Your shameful dress and immodest ornament accuse you; nor can you be counted now among Christ's maidens and virgins, since you live in such a manner as to make yourselves objects of desire" (*The Ante-Nicene Fathers,* Vol. V).

In spite of such efforts, though, by the third century A.D. the wearing of rings was becoming an increasing problem even among women who called themselves Christian.

Profaning the Ring

A third reason why there was opposition to ring wearing, particularly the wedding ring, was the frequency of misuse.

William Jones, in his book *Finger-Ring Lore,* wrote in 1890, "In old times rings of rushes were used for immoral purposes, not only in England, but in France." He continued, "The 'heathenish origin,' as it was termed, of the wedding ring, led during the Commonwealth to the abolition of its use during weddings, and is thus referred to in Butler's 'Hudibras'—

> Others were for abolishing
>   That tool of matrimony, a ring,
> With which the unsanctified bridegroom
>   Is marry'd only to a thumb*
> (As wise as ringing of a pig,
>   That used to break up ground and dig).
> The bride to nothing but her will
>   That nulls the after-marriage still.

"This 'heathenish origin' may have been derived from the supposition that the ring was regarded as a kind of phylactery, or charm, and to have been introduced in imitation of the ring worn by the bishops."

Jones thus shows that even in secular England there was strong opposition to wearing of the wedding ring for at least three reasons: it was of heathenish origin; it was used as a cover-up for clandestine sexual affairs; and it was no assurance that the marriage would be a success.

The misuse of wedding rings did not cease in that ancient day. As recently as June 18, 1951, an article in *LIFE* declared that most wedding rings manufactured in the United States are used for immoral purposes, and that the symbolism of the ring is promoted by commercial interests because of a profit motive.

The Puritan Failure

The Puritans of England, including some Baptists, Congregationalists, and Quakers, sought during the 16th and 17th centuries to free religion of Roman influence and to bring a revival of holy living. One of their efforts was to place a ban on the ring.

---

*Some early wedding rings were placed on the thumb.

Like earlier endeavors to the same purpose it eventually came to an unfruitful end. William Jones wrote as follows: " 'Though the Puritans,' remarks Mr. Jeaffreson, in his 'Brides and Bridals,' 'prohibited and preached against the ring, to the injury of goldsmiths, and the wrath of ring-wearing matrons, they did not succeed in abolishing the tool . . .' " *(Ibid.).*

There may be some people who feel that because the wedding ring is so generally accepted in British circles today it has always been that way. The foregoing information should dispel that belief, for the ring which was banned by the Puritans was specifically the wedding ring.

The Mennonite Position

The Mennonites and their forerunners, the Anabaptists, have historically taken a strong position against superfluous and jeweled apparel. A special session of the Mennonite General Conference of 1944 declared, "That our expressed standards on the doctrine of nonconformity to the world, relating to . . . the wearing of jewelry (including wedding rings), attendance at movies and theaters, be made a test of fellowship in communion and, if persisted in, be made a test of membership" (quoted in Wilbur D. Kropf, *Jewelry and the Wedding Band*).

The Holiness Movement and the Ring

Wesley's Position

In early England there was opposition to the wedding ring, both from secular government circles and the religious bodies. The Puritans, as was pointed out in the last discussion, made a strong prohibitive effort which eventually failed. John Wesley, who came not long after the height of Puritanism, likewise stood against the growing custom. He also used the teaching of Paul in Timothy 2:9, 10 as a basis for his position. Here is one of his discourses on the subject, found in his article, "Advice to the People called Methodists, With Regard to Dress":

> I "exhort all those who desire me to watch over their souls," Wear no gold . . . no pearls, or precious stones; use no curling of hair, or costly apparel, how grave soever. . . . I do not advise women to wear rings, ear-rings, necklaces. . . . It is true, [speaking of shining buckles, etc.] these are little, very little things, which are not worth defending; therefore, give them up, let them drop, throw them away without another word; else, a little needle may cause much pain in

your flesh, a little self-indulgence much hurt to your soul (*Works,* Vol. XI).

The Methodist societies were called Bands. In answer to a question concerning them, "Should we insist on the Band rules, particularly with regard to dress?" Wesley wrote,

> By all means. This is no time to give any encouragement to superfluity of apparel. Therefore give no Band-tickets to any till they have left off superfluous ornaments. In order to do this. (1.) Let every assistant read the "Thoughts upon Dress" at least once a year, and in every large society. . . . (3.) Allow no exempt case, not even of a married woman. Better one suffer than many" (Vol. VIII).

From his writings it does not appear that Clarke was as strongly opposed to rings as Wesley was. Nevertheless he argued for simplicity in dress and adornment, for this reason:

> I think it has its reason in the case itself, and in the feelings and apprehensions of the spouse who produces [the ring]. He has chosen, according to his feelings one whom he esteems the most perfect of her kind: she is to him superior to every other female, adorned with every charm. To use then, in this state of the case, any adornment, would be a tacit confession that her person was defective, and needed something to set it off, and must be more or less dependent on the feeble aid of dress *(Clarke's Christian Theology).*

Modern Methodism

The influence of Wesley was strong and enduring, and had an impact on Methodist teaching for many years. Nevertheless, there was a gradual relaxation of the principles of separation from the world, until like other efforts that were finally abandoned, there remained no restriction to wearing of jewelry.

A Methodist historian has written as follows:

While after the General Rules were given by Wesley, no additional formalized statement of personal disciplines to be observed was developed in Methodism . . . similar traditions with reference to proper conduct for church members developed which were so pronounced as to have strong binding effect. Thinking has changed some among United Methodists particularly at the point of some things once termed "worldly," but it is still expected that United Methodists shall be a people committed to purity of life, sobriety, self-control, and the highest standards of personal conduct (Roy H. Short, *United Methodism in Theory and Practice*).

The present writer can still remember statements of regret made by some of the holy men who lived back in the day when the Methodists were changing their position about what was "once" termed "worldly." That abandonment of separation was one of the strong motivating forces which brought into existence so many new holiness bodies during the latter part of the 19th century. They were committed afresh to the purity of the body of Christ, and to a scriptural application of principles of separation from the world.

The Holiness Position and the Ring

The Beginnings

When the Methodist Church began to relax its position about separation from the world, and for this and other reasons a number of newly-formed holiness groups appeared, they were generally strong and clear-cut about their principles of separation. During World War II this writer had occasion to visit a number of holiness churches in various parts of the United States—Free Methodist, Nazarene, Pilgrim Holiness, Church of God (Holiness), and others—and found them alike conservative in matters of dress and adornment. At that time a distinctive of most any truly holiness church was its mark of modesty, including abstinence from jewelry and the wedding ring.

Many years ago Rev. A. L. Vess wrote,

> Whatever else may be affirmed or denied, one thing is certain: there *was* a time when the jewelry question was settled in the Holiness movement. There was no question as to our stand on the subject, not

even the wedding ring was excepted. The wedding band was just classed with all other kinds of jewelry, and considered the property of formal churches and of the world *(The Loophole)*.

Articles are available from the early issues of *The Free Methodist, The Wesleyan Methodist, The Pilgrim Holiness Advocate, The Herald of Holiness,* and *The Church Herald and Holiness Banner,* which show the clear-cut position of the respective bodies toward the wedding ring.

From *The Free Methodist*

An article taken from *The Free Methodist* has been reprinted without date under the title "Light on the Wedding Ring." The writer, Rev. E. B. Annable, made a sane and fervent appeal for continued abstinence from ring wearing.

> In any vital matter [the wedding ring] is no evidence at all, because the ring is no proof of actual marriage. A plain band ring may easily be obtained and worn by anyone wishing to pass for married. . . . Again, a married person may still more easily take off his or her ring, if wishing for any reason to appear unmarried. . . . Only one conclusion is possible on this point: the wedding ring is a generally accepted badge of marriage, but it is no proof of it.

He proceeded to give strong scriptural support for abstinence.

From *The Herald of Holiness*

Following are two quotations from the "Question Box" section of *The Herald of Holiness,* written by the editor:

> Q. Do you think it wrong for a Christian to wear a wedding band?
> A. In a country like our own where no such custom [the requirement of rings] is universally observed, and in the case of people whose children about the table constitute the very finest wedding ring, and whose conduct proves their fidelity to one partner in

life, it seems to me that there is no reasonable excuse for violating the Scriptures' prohibition of wearing gold and noticeable apparel (Dec. 12, 1924).

Q. Do you think our pastors should perform wedding ceremonies, using the wedding ring?

A. No. A good many Methodist preachers, including at least one of the bishops, refuse to use the ring ceremony on the ground that it is out of harmony with the letter and spirit of the Methodist discipline to do so. And our Manual is as strong on the wearing of jewelry as the Methodist Discipline, and our preachers and our preaching ought to be as consistent as the Methodists—the best Methodists" (July 14, 1926).

The Nazarene Manual, it may be added, based its position on the Scriptures, and not just on what other bodies were doing.

The Change

By the mid-1940's the teachers of the Church of the Nazarene had decided to relax their position on separation from the world as a means of promoting more rapid growth of the denomination. While the statement in the Manual did not change, the application of the Scriptures to the wearing of jewelry was relaxed. The editor answered in the "Question Box," July 17, 1950:

Q. When I was converted and joined the Church of the Nazarene, we were not supposed to wear gold rings on our fingers. . . . But now we see people in our movement wearing diamond rings, and ring ceremonies are being used in some of our weddings. This leaves some of us in a very embarrassing position. What is the right thing?

A. This statement [quoted from the Manual] has never been interpreted in exactly the same way, even by the best members of the Church of the Nazarene.

I must say that I am disturbed about a growing laxity on the part of some of our people as to the matter of dress. I think there is grave danger along this line. We must not substitute outward adornment for the inward adornment of the spirit.

Some Objections Considered

"No Ornament"

There are many people who insist that the wearing of a simple wedding band is not an ornament, and not adornment; therefore it is not forbidden by the writings of Paul and Peter. Here is a response by Rev. E. B. Annable:

> We do not doubt that a host of devout women have worn the ring purely as a token of loyal marriage, who would not put on other ornamental jewelry.
> . . .
> But while their motives are pure, we believe their practice was in error. Why? Because we have witnessed that their less devout neighbors, relatives, and often their own children, were bold to put on more and more "badges," class rings, signet rings, lockets, keepsakes, etc. The camel's nose was permitted in the tent (as in the old fable), and that let in the whole camel at

last! Not an ornament? Then neither is a glittering watch chain, breastpin, or what-have-you. Not an ornament? Then why risk your godly example by wearing it? Why not let your marriage certificate (which costs almost nothing) be your marriage evidence, which has none of the several risks of the ring? But the persistence with which you cling to the ring seems to betray a fondness for the custom, and a deep-seated unwillingness to be thought unfashionable, more than the fear of being thought unmarried ("Light on the Wedding Ring," an undated booklet).

"Not Entirely Forbidden"

A variation of the above argument relates to I Peter 3:3, "Whose adorning let it not be that outward adorning of plaiting the hair, and of wearing of gold, or of putting on of apparel." It is asserted that this teaches only moderation in use of jewelry, and not total abstinence; for if it teaches total abstinence of jewelry, then it also applies total abstinence to "putting on of apparel." This has an appearance of reason until it is carefully examined.

J. B. Smith, in an appendix to his book, *The Revelation of Jesus Christ,* shows that whenever Peter used this particular form of the expression "not . . . but . . ." (*ou alla*, in Greek) it means a total exclusion of the one in favor of the other. For example, it is used in his expressions, "Ye were *not* redeemed with corruptible things . . . *but* with the precious blood of Christ" (1 Peter 1:18, 19) and "Being born again, *not* of corruptible seed, but of incorruptible, by the word of God" (1:23). The pair of words is used nearly ten times in the two epistles, and every other place than the passage under consideration it obviously represents a total exclusion of the first item in favor of the second. It is only reasonable to interpret the passage on jewelry in the same way.

Concerning the "putting on of apparel," the word used is not that for ordinary dress, as Paul used in I Timothy 2:9, "In like manner also, that women adorn themselves in modest apparel, with shamefacedness and sobriety; not with broided hair, or gold, or pearls, or costly array." The words "modest apparel" use a different Greek term from the one Peter used for "apparel." They literally mean "a let-down garment," or a garment that covers. They refer to a simple and complete dress or robe.

Peter's term for "apparel" is the same which Paul used in the expression "costly array." It plainly refers to extravagant dress. So the two sacred writers were in agreement: dress should be modest, but not extravagant. The recent argument that Peter is just teaching moderation in jewelry as in dress is totally amiss.

A Needed Protection

It is commonly argued that a married woman needs the ring as a protection against the advances of unprincipled men. Here is a sensible response:

> Where . . . is the real value of the emblem in a test? Would it save an employer from hiring a married woman contrary to rules, if all she needs to do is slip her ring off while at the factory, store, or office? Also, would her ring "protect" a married woman from insult or attack, if a man really took occasion to attack her? Again, would a ring, worn falsely, "protect" a rooming-house manager from giving "her" a room with "him" to whom she had no right? . . .
>
> What, then, is the real protection of the married in public business or society? There are but two necessary things. The first is the marriage certificate. . . .
>
> Another protection—safe for both the married and the single—is good, old-fashioned virtue reflected in clean, honest faces, and in modesty of conduct and of appearance. This is real protection. It does not need rings or any other sign or badge to keep off intruders (Annabel, *Ibid.*).

Another Objection

"The Bible Allowed It"

Three common objections to the prohibition of rings were considered in the last discussion. Another common one is this: "The Bible records instances of ring wearing, and it adds no condemnation to the practice. Why then should it be condemned today?"

That is a fair question, and it deserves a fair answer. It is true that there are cases recorded in the Bible where not only rings, but other forms of jewelry as well, were worn, and no condemnation is added to the immediate context. One example is that of Abraham's servant who went to seek a wife for Isaac. "And it came to pass . . . that the man took a golden earring of half a shekel weight. and two bracelets for her hands of ten shekels weight of gold" (Gen. 24:22).

It is well to remember two facts here: first, this incident occurred before God had given any condemnation of wearing jewelry on the flesh, at least so far as the written record indicates; second, the Lord "winked at" some things in those days which He later condemned.

The Apostle's Explanation

It has already been shown that God designed precious jewels to portray His own beauty, holiness, and eternity. Wherever His presence was to be manifested, there were the beauty of these stones and metals. It was easy for people to forget the invisible God and set their affections on the visible symbols. Soon they were making the jewels and precious metals into objects of worship and calling them gods.

Paul referred to this inclination when he said that they "changed the glory of the uncorruptible God into an image made like to corruptible man. . . . Who changed the truth of God into a lie, and worshipped and served the creature more than the Creator, who is blessed for ever" (Rom. 1:23, 25).

The apostle observed the idolatry of Athens and condemned it in these words: "We ought not to think that the Godhead is like unto gold, or silver, or stone, graven by art and man's device. And the times of this ignorance God winked at: but now commandeth all men every where to repent" (Acts 17:29, 30). Observe that it was specifically one of the misuses of jewelry—using it to fashion objects of worship—that God had formerly "winked at," but now commands men to repent of the same. The fact that God allowed such a misuse at an ancient, Old Testament date, does not mean that He always permits it. The emphatic condemnations which later occur, even in the Old Testament, are enough to show that God did not approve the practice just because He "winked at" it.

Joseph's Ring

"And Pharaoh took off his ring from his hand, and put it upon Joseph's hand, and arrayed him in vestures of fine linen, and put a gold chain about his neck" (Gen. 41:42). The first discussion of this series referred to this incident, with an explanation of the function of a signet ring: it was a means of certifying documents with kingly authority.

The fact that God did not condemn the practice is explained in the same way as the foregoing incident. He allowed what was traditional at the time, and waited until a later time to express His will in the matter.

God's Beauty on His Bride

Israel was considered to be the bride of Jehovah. He sought her as an unworthy, abandoned child, washed her, and entered into a covenant of marriage with her. In Ezekiel 16:11-17 He explained, "I decked thee also with ornaments, and I put bracelets upon thy hands. and a chain on thy neck. And I put a jewel on thy forehead, and earrings in thine ears, and a beautiful crown upon thine head. Thus wast thou decked with gold and silver. . . . And thy renown went forth among the heathen for thy beauty: for it was perfect through my comeliness, which I had put upon thee, saith the Lord God. But thou didst trust in thine own beauty, and playedst the harlot. . . . Thou hast also taken thy fair jewels of my gold and of my silver, which I had given thee, and madest to thyself images of men."

This is highly figurative language, of course. Adam Clarke explained as follows, with other commentators agreeing: "By this wretched infant, the low estate of the Jewish nation in its origin is pointed out . . . by her being decked out and ornamented, her Tabernacle service and religious ordinances; by her betrothing and consequent marriage, the covenant which God made with the Jews."

The Chaldee *Targum* rendered its spiritual interpretation thus: "I gave the ark of my covenant to be among you, and the cloud of my glory overshadowed you, and the angel of my presence led you in the way." Whereas the heathen literally put jewels on the flesh, God placed *His own comeliness* upon His people (v. 14).

The writings of Paul and Peter indicate God's permanent will for His people is just that: whereas people of the world identify marriage with fleshly decorations, He wants holy women to refrain from the same and make their adornment His own gift of a meek and quiet spirit (I Tim. 2:8-10; I Peter 3:3, 4).

The Prodigal

A New Testament Case

Persons who are looking for justification in wearing of jewelry often give the case of the prodigal son as evidence that Jesus allowed it. It was He who told the story and expressed the words of the father, "Bring forth the best robe, and put it on him; and put a ring on his hand, and shoes on his feet: and bring hither the fatted calf, and kill it; and let us eat, and be merry" (Luke 15:22, 23).

In this case, as in Old Testament examples, a story was told which drew upon common customs of the day, and a spiritual interpretation was made. The telling of such a story in order to make spiritual truth plain does not mean that every element in the story is morally justified. Jesus did not authorize the eating of fat, a practice forbidden in the Old Testament (Lev. 3:17), just because the fatted calf was to be eaten in His story. He did not authorize the wearing of elaborate robes, a practice which Paul condemned (I Tim. 2:9), just because in His story the son was clothed in the best robe. The story is a figure—a parable—which portrays spiritual truth. The truth is that "there is joy in the presence of the angels of God over one sinner that repenteth," a truth illustrated three times in this one chapter. So the story does not authorize ring wearing for the followers of Jesus.

Summary

At considerable length a review of the Bible and history concerning wearing of jewelry has been presented, with special reference to the wedding ring. The material may be briefly summarized as follows.

God placed these precious items in the natural world as fitting illustrations of His own holy character, for they display purity, beauty, serviceability, and durability. Because of their value, gems and precious metals served as money in the ancient world, even as they form the basis of monetary value in many places today.

The first being to take upon himself the beauty of God's "stones of fire," and to fall thereby, was Satan, if as is commonly believed Ezekiel 28:12-17 refers to his fall from heaven. His heart was lifted up because of his beauty; he covered himself with the sardius, the topaz, the diamond, and other stones; therefore God cast him down from his high place.

Satan always seeks to inject into the lives of people the elements of his own disposition: pride, deception, rebellion, unbelief, and others. It is no wonder that very early in human history there arose an apparently insatiable desire to put precious stones and precious metals on the flesh as items of personal adornment. The secular writer Kunz was quoted earlier: "The wearing of rings as ornaments for the hand requires no explanation in view of innate love of adornment shown from the very earliest periods of human history" *(Rings for the Finger)*. Encyclopedia Britannica adds, "Over the years the limited jewelry forms of prehistoric times multiplied until they included ornaments for every part of the body" (15th ed., Vol. 10).

Restrictions Fail

God often placed restrictions on the misuse of jewelry, including the wearing of rings (Num. 31:50-54, Isa. 3:21, etc.).

Secular nations and religious bodies enacted legislation to keep the human propensity for jewelry in check. This included the Jews, Romans, British, Roman Catholics, Anabaptists, Puritans, Methodists, and numerous holiness bodies. Time and again, however, the human insistence on wearing such items became so strong that the prohibitions were overridden and finally canceled or ignored.

The early Methodist movement started with a strong prohibition of all jewelry, including the wedding ring. After many years, the restriction was nullified. Partly because of this the recent holiness bodies had their origin. Although there were some minor exceptions, these bodies stood quite unitedly in the Methodist tradition and forbade ring wearing, using Scripture as the basis for such prohibition.

By the mid-20th century these holiness bodies were experiencing the same wave of popular opposition to any such prohibition, and one by one they removed them. So what is commonly called the "conservative holiness movement" arose, again purposing to maintain careful, scriptural separation from the world, including abstinence from all jewelry.

It remains to be seen whether this recent movement will do any better than the former ones in resisting the mysterious, forceful urge to put some of God's jewels on human flesh.

Treasures of God's Heart and Hand

The Priest's Breastplate

When the high priest went into the Temple to perform his service before the Lord, one of the items of his apparel was the breastplate with its twelve settings of precious stones. Although there is some problem in determining the equivalence between the terms used in the Bible and modern classification, here is a likely comparison, showing what may have been the colors involved:

1. Sardius, probably modern ruby: a ruddy red color
2. Topaz, chrysolite: green or yellow
3. Carbuncle, or garnet: reddish or possibly clear
4. Emerald: bright green
5. Sapphire, lapis Lazuli: sky blue
6. Diamond, possibly the onyx: sparkling clear or black and white
7. Ligure, maybe the jacinth: yellow or orange

8. Agate: many hues, mostly golden green
9. Amethyst: variable from strong blue to deep purple or rose color
10. Beryl: bluish green or yellow
11. Onyx, the malachite: perhaps white and brown bands, on a sky-colored background
12. Jasper: many colors, perhaps mostly green or brown

Our Great High Priest

Those stones on the breastplate represented the twelve tribes of Israel. The stones were borne over the heart of the priest as he went into the Temple, and once a year into the Holiest before the Lord. In a similar way our High Priest, Jesus Christ, bears His people on His heart as He ministers in the heavenly sanctuary. Hebrews 9:24 says, "Christ is not entered into the holy places made with hands, which are the figures of the true; but into heaven itself, now to appear in the presence of God for us." (So far as the Bible record indicates, everything Christ has done since His ascension is for His people on earth!) Today Jesus has us on His heart, as He intercedes for us!

Many Hues in the Light

The lapidary shaped those stones to make them suitable for the priest's breastplate. Imagine the beauty when all of them reflected the light of the candlesticks or the shekinah of God's glory! There were most all of the rainbow colors, scintillating in the flickering lights of the Tabernacle, or later the Temple.

Now God is preparing some jewels to adorn His eternal habitation. "A book of remembrance was written before him for them that feared the Lord, and that thought upon his name. And they shall be mine, saith the Lord of hosts, in that day when I make up my jewels; and I will spare them, as a man spareth his own son that serveth him" (Mal. 3:16, 17). Note the emphases on service, communion, reverence, and meditation.

Jewels represent God's people who are being prepared for His eternal habitations, to grace His presence. Not all of them are radiantly colorful; some stones were less brilliant than others. Likewise, not all people have sparkling, outgoing personalities. Some incline to be somber, others effervescent and buoyant. Once temperaments were thought to be of four basic types: sanguine, (from blood and a ruddy color), a cheerful, sturdy type; choleric (from bile, a yellow color), aggressive, hot-tempered; phlegmatic (from a word for flame, indicating blackness), the slow, firm, imperturbable type; and melancholy (dark in color), indicating a pensive, thoughtful type.

In recent years this classification has been revived, but it is believed that there are overlaps of the various types, so there are more than four simple ones. Surely there are as many personality types as there were stones on the priest's breastplate.

Whatever our type may be, we can be glad we are borne on the heart of our Great High Priest. He is cutting, grinding, and polishing us for our place in the Kingdom.

A Signet on God's Hand

Haggai's prophecy closes with a word concerning Zerubbabel: "In that day, saith the Lord of hosts, will I take thee, O Zerubbabel, my servant, the son of Shealtiel, saith the Lord, and will make thee as a signet: for I have chosen thee, saith the Lord of hosts."

The signet was a sign of authority in those days. From their Syrian backgrounds the prophets often referred to the signet. It was a cylinder with a cord through it, placed around the hand. A king used it to transpose his seal to important documents. Spiritually it signifies at least two things:

First, it often bore the image of the king. God would make a man to bear His image. He is still doing that; He is working at the job for all of His people.

Second, it was an item of service, not of show. It was to convey that image to something else. "My servant," God called the man. That is also what He wants to make of all believers. We are to serve; we are to communicate His image to the lives of others.

Not only Zerubbabel, but every one of us, can be one of God's signets if we will bear the polishing and carry His image!

www.ingramcontent.com/pod-product-compliance
Lightning Source LLC
Chambersburg PA
CBHW071313040426
42444CB00009B/2000